Cambridge Elements

Elements in Cognitive Linguistics
edited by
Sarah Duffy
Northumbria University
Nick Riches
Newcastle University

LINGUISTIC SYNESTHESIA

A Meta-analysis

Bodo Winter
University of Birmingham

Francesca Strik-Lievers
University of Genoa

Shaftesbury Road, Cambridge CB2 8EA, United Kingdom

One Liberty Plaza, 20th Floor, New York, NY 10006, USA

477 Williamstown Road, Port Melbourne, VIC 3207, Australia

314–321, 3rd Floor, Plot 3, Splendor Forum, Jasola District Centre, New Delhi – 110025, India

103 Penang Road, #05–06/07, Visioncrest Commercial, Singapore 238467

Cambridge University Press is part of Cambridge University Press & Assessment, a department of the University of Cambridge.

We share the University's mission to contribute to society through the pursuit of education, learning and research at the highest international levels of excellence.

www.cambridge.org
Information on this title: www.cambridge.org/9781009519168

DOI: 10.1017/9781009519182

© Bodo Winter and Francesca Strik-Lievers 2025

This publication is in copyright. Subject to statutory exception and to the provisions of relevant collective licensing agreements, no reproduction of any part may take place without the written permission of Cambridge University Press & Assessment.

When citing this work, please include a reference to the DOI 10.1017/9781009519182

First published 2025

A catalogue record for this publication is available from the British Library

ISBN 978-1-009-51916-8 Hardback
ISBN 978-1-009-51914-4 Paperback
ISSN 2633-3325 (online)
ISSN 2633-3317 (print)

Cambridge University Press & Assessment has no responsibility for the persistence or accuracy of URLs for external or third-party internet websites referred to in this publication and does not guarantee that any content on such websites is, or will remain, accurate or appropriate.

For EU product safety concerns, contact us at Calle de José Abascal, 56, 1°, 28003 Madrid, Spain, or email eugpsr@cambridge.org

Linguistic Synesthesia

A Meta-analysis

Elements in Cognitive Linguistics

DOI: 10.1017/9781009519182
First published online: June 2025

Bodo Winter
University of Birmingham

Francesca Strik-Lievers
University of Genoa

Author for correspondence: Bodo Winter, b.winter@bham.ac.uk

Abstract: Linguistic synesthesias combine different senses, as in English *smooth melody* (touch→sound). For nearly a century, researchers have gathered data that have been interpreted as supporting the notion of a hierarchical ordering of the senses. According to this proposal, expressions map the presumed-to-be "lower" senses of touch, taste, and smell onto the presumed-to-be "higher" senses of sound and sight. Here, this proposal is tested in the first-ever meta-analysis of linguistic synesthesias, combining thirty-eight datasets from fourteen different languages. The authors demonstrate that clear patterns emerge from the data, but many such patterns are inconsistent with the notion of a linear hierarchical order or a simple lower/higher divide of the senses. This calls for a shift in what theories are considered to be viable for explaining asymmetries between the senses in linguistic synesthesia.

Keywords: perception, sensory language, metaphor, embodied cognition, synesthesia

© Bodo Winter and Francesca Strik-Lievers 2025

ISBNs: 9781009519168 (HB), 9781009519144 (PB), 9781009519182 (OC)
ISSNs: 2633-3325 (online), 2633-3317 (print)

Contents

1. Introduction — 1
2. Why a Meta-Analysis of Linguistic Synesthesia Is Needed — 6
3. The Hierarchy of the Senses: Evidence and Theory — 10
4. Methods — 20
5. Analysis #1: Hierarchy Congruency — 31
6. Analysis #2: Source/Target Ratios — 37
7. Analysis #3: Pairwise Asymmetry — 42
8. Analysis #4: Specific Mappings — 44
9. Discussion — 47
10. Conclusion and Outlook for Future Research on Linguistic Synesthesia — 61

References — 62

1 Introduction

We come to experience the world via our senses, traditionally divided into sight, sound, touch, taste, and smell. The senses do not live in isolation but are deeply connected. Perceptual psychology provides ample evidence for interactions between the senses, such as illusions, where one sense can change what the other one perceives. In the double flash illusion, for example, a single light flash (sight) accompanied by two beeps (sound) makes people see two light flashes (Shams et al., 2000). There also is evidence for a variety of crossmodal correspondences (Spence, 2011), such as people matching higher-pitched sounds to brighter images (e.g, Marks, 1974) and lower-pitched sounds to rounder shapes (e.g., O'Boyle & Tarte, 1980). Finally, there is a phenomenon called synesthesia, rare in the general population (Deroy & Spence, 2013; Simner et al., 2006, 2009), where certain individuals have vivid atypical sensory experiences often involving connections between the senses, such as automatically seeing colors when hearing particular sounds.

Just as the senses are richly interwoven in perception, they are also deeply connected in language (e.g., Alvarado et al., 2024; Classen, 1993, Ch. 3; Winter, 2019a). The rare phenomenon of synesthesia lends its name to linguistic synesthesia, otherwise known as synesthetic metaphor[1] (key references in the annotated bibliography Strik-Lievers, 2023). Linguistic synesthesias combine linguistic expressions that are strongly associated with different modalities, thus generating a conflict between separate sensory concepts (Strik-Lievers, 2017). For example, in the English adjective-noun pair *smooth melody*, the adjective is associated with touch, but it modifies a noun that describes an auditory concept. Linguistic synesthesias are generally seen as involving a metaphorical transfer *from* one sense (source) *to* the sense the expression is about (target) (but see Paradis & Eeg-Olofsson, 2013; Rakova, 2003; Winter, 2019a, 2019b). In adjective-noun pairs such as *smooth melody,* the noun is the head of a noun phrase, and ultimately what the phrase is about. Under a metaphorical analysis, this noun is seen as the target of the intersensory transfer, whereas the modifying adjective is seen as the source. The phrase *smooth melody* would then be characterized as featuring a touch→sound (source→target) transfer. Syntactic configurations other than adjective-noun pairs can usually be analyzed in the

---

[1] This team of authors has different views on the nature of linguistic synesthesias, with one author seeing them as metaphors (Strik-Lievers, 2017), the other one seeing them as literal expressions (Winter, 2019b). For the topic of this study, this theoretical issue is irrelevant. The asymmetries that are the focus of this Element can be described irrespective of how the expressions are classified; both metaphorical projection and contextual modification of literal expressions can model asymmetries (cf. discussion in Winter, 2019a, pp. 102–103). We chose to adopt the label "linguistic synesthesia" here as it is commonly employed in the literature and does not commit ourselves to a particular interpretation, unlike the equally frequent "synesthetic metaphor."

same way, in which case the target always relates to the sensory modality the expression is about, whereas the modality conflicting with it is the source. For instance, the copular clause *This melody is smooth* would be treated as also featuring a touch→sound transfer.

Starting with Stephen Ullmann (1937, 1945, 1946, 1947, 1959[1951]), many researchers have noted that there are striking patterns in linguistic synesthesias within individual languages as well as across languages, specifically with respect to which senses are more likely to be combined with which others, and whether a sense tends to be a source or a target (e.g., Day, 1996; Kumcu, 2021; Ronga et al., 2012; Shen, 1997; Strik-Lievers, 2015; Winter, 2019a; Zhao et al., 2019). For example, in adjective-noun pairs, researchers have noted that touch (source) adjectives are commonly combined with auditory (target) nouns (e.g., *smooth melody, rough/abrasive/hard/blunt sound*, etc.), but the reverse happens very rarely, that is, auditory adjectives such as *loud*, *quiet*, or *squealing* rarely modify tactile nouns such as *touch* or *feeling*. This asymmetry between sound and touch has been found in a number of studies on different languages (e.g., Day, 1996; Kumcu, 2021; Ronga et al., 2012; Shen, 1997; Strik-Lievers, 2015; Ullmann, 1959; Winter, 2019a; Zhao et al., 2019).

Ullmann paved the way for future investigations of linguistic synesthesia. Based on the analysis of literary texts in French, Hungarian, and English, he established the following generalizations about linguistic synesthesia (1959, pp. 280–283):

(i) Intersensory transfers tend to go from "lower" to "higher" modalities
(ii) Touch is the most common source modality
(iii) Sound is the most common target modality

Later work reinterpreted Ullmann's generalizations in the context of implicational hierarchies in linguistic typology, with Viberg (1983) being the first to formulate the following linear representation (p. 159):

(iv) touch > heat > taste > scent > sound > sight

As a Western-European scholar, it is perhaps no surprise that already in his earliest paper, Ullmann (1937) relied on the Western cultural idea that hearing and especially sight are more advanced than touch, taste, or smell (Classen, 1993). The hierarchy above could then be characterized in terms of the senses being sorted from "lower" to "higher," with the former mapping onto the latter more likely than the reverse. Or, in other words, presumed-to-be lower senses are common sources in linguistic synesthesia; presumed-to-be higher senses are common targets. Perhaps aided through Viberg's representation, Ullmann's generalizations have later often been interpreted as a hierarchy that is "linear" (Jo, 2022, p. 284; Kumcu, 2021, p. 241; Zhong et al., 2023, p. 3). Here, we refer to any proposal that assumes either a linear ordering or a binary divide between the lower and higher senses as "the hierarchy of the senses," notwithstanding important differences between theoretical proposals (for discussion, see Shinohara & Nakayama, 2011; Winter, 2019a, Ch. 8). We will deal with different versions of the hierarchy later in this study.

Linguistic synesthesias have been studied both experimentally and observationally. In observational studies, such as those by Ullmann and the others mentioned above, the evidence consists in the frequency with which specific combinations of the senses appear in texts or dictionaries, and the prevalence of each sense as a source versus as a target. On the other hand, experimental studies (Fishman, 2022; Nakamura et al., 2010; Sakamoto & Utsumi, 2014; Shen & Gil, 2008; Shinohara & Nakayama, 2011; Werning et al., 2006; Winter & Strik-Lievers, 2023; Zhong et al., 2023) use linguistic synesthesias as stimuli.[2] For example, Shen and Aisenman (2008) show that Hebrew linguistic synesthesias aligning with the hierarchy of the senses, such as *sweet fragrance* (taste→smell), are judged to be more natural and are more easily retained in memory than those conflicting with the hierarchy, such as *fragrant sweetness* (smell→taste). Similar results come from Shinohara and Nakayama (2011), who show that synesthetic adjective-noun phrases in Japanese that conform to the hierarchy are judged to be more understandable than those phrases that violate the hierarchy. Similarly, German speakers tested by Werning et al. (2006) rate hierarchy-congruent synesthesias as more accessible than incongruent ones. With both sources of evidence – experiments and observational studies – pointing toward a similar set of asymmetries between the senses, such as between sound and touch, the question naturally arises: What explains these asymmetries? *Why* do so many patterns look, at first sight, like they follow a hierarchy of the senses?

Explanations for the hierarchy abound (for reviews, see Fishman, 2022; Winter, 2019a, Ch. 9), with Williams (1976) being the first prominent paper to speculate that asymmetries in linguistic synesthesia may stem from extralinguistic asymmetries between the senses, in his case, biological asymmetries. He observed that the way the senses relate in his data loosely parallels the

---

[2] It is worth pointing out that observational and experimental evidence for the hierarchy of the senses cannot be treated as independent from each other, as experiments in this space are inherently language-based. Even in studies where stimuli are novel instances of linguistic synesthesia, not attested in corpora, the frequency of use of the individual lexemes, together with other linguistic features, can influence outcomes. Werning et al. (2006), for instance, show that accessibility ratings depend not only on the sensory modality of the lexemes but also on their corpus frequency and morphological features, with more frequent and nonderived adjectives enhancing the accessibility of the synesthetic expressions in which they appear (see also Winter & Strik-Lievers, 2023).

development of the senses in human phylogenetic evolution as well as in the ontogenetic maturation of the senses in infants, with touch being an evolutionarily ancient sensory modality that is already active at birth and the other senses sequentially emerging thereafter. Thus, Williams (1976) seeks to explain observations about asymmetries between sensory terms *in language* with something that is external to language, such as biological facts about perception.

Seeking a direct link between language and language-external facts also characterizes some strands of modern work on linguistic synesthesia, such as proposals which see Ullmann's generalizations from the perspective of embodiment (e.g., Zhao et al., 2019, 2022). The embodied cognition framework – not without its fair share of critics (e.g., Goldinger et al., 2016; Hickok, 2014; Leshinskaya & Caramazza, 2016; Mahon & Caramazza, 2008; Mahon & Hickok, 2016; Morey et al., 2021) – emphasizes the role of low-level processes involving perception and action in higher-level processes such as language and cognition. In the context of linguistic synesthesia, researchers have attempted to distinguish the senses in terms of the "degree of embodiment" (Zhong et al., 2023, p. 2), or variously in terms of how the senses differ with reference to notions such as "accessibility" or "concreteness" (Shen, 1997; Shen & Aisenman, 2008; Shen & Cohen, 1998; Shen & Gadir, 2009; Shen & Gil, 2008). Shen (1997, pp. 54–55), for example, suggests that sensory modalities involving direct contact with the source of the stimulus, such as touch, are more accessible than those not involving contact, like sight. Shen and colleagues also characterize touch and, to a lesser extent, taste and smell as more "concrete" senses than hearing and sight (Shen & Cohen, 1998; Shen & Gil, 2008), and this difference in "concreteness" is supposed to lie behind the observed asymmetries between the senses in language.

These proposals are situated within cognitive linguistics and explicitly link the hierarchy of linguistic synesthesia to conceptual metaphor theory, the general proposal that metaphors are rooted in facts about human cognition, specifically the tendency to think and talk about the abstract in terms of the concrete (Gibbs, 1994; Kövecses, 2002; Lakoff & Johnson, 1980, 1999). With other biological or perceptually grounded explanations, these proposals share the view that factors external to language govern what senses form likely sources or targets. This has parallels with the typological literature on how sensory meanings are connected in the semantics of perception verbs across languages, where Viberg (1983) has observed comparable hierarchical tendencies that are also often understood to be at least partially grounded in facts about human perception (Evans & Wilkins, 2000; Viberg, 2001).

Alongside approaches that seek language-external explanations, such as "embodiment," there are studies that have provided evidence for language-internal factors determining some of the observed asymmetries. For example, Strik-Lievers (2015) focused on the internal composition of the sensory vocabulary with respect to part-of-speech categories (cf. Strik-Lievers & Winter, 2018), showing that in her data, those senses that are more lexically differentiated in the adjectival domain also feature more commonly as sources. This helps explain why sight→sound expressions (e.g., *bright sound*) are more common than sound→sight expressions: the word list used by Strik-Lievers (2015) features more adjectives for sight than sound, and given this distribution, sight has a greater opportunity to act as a source. Winter (2019a) provided additional evidence that the composition of the sensory vocabulary can help explain asymmetries observed in corpus data. He also provided empirical evidence for three other lexical factors: word frequency, iconicity, and emotional valence. For example, adjectives that are relatively more emotional are more likely to be used as sources in linguistic synesthesia, which helps explain why taste commonly features as source (e.g., *sweet melody*), given that taste vocabulary has strong emotional connotations (Bagli, 2017; Winter, 2016). Uncovering another lexical factor that may play a role in linguistic synesthesia, Petersen et al. (2008) provide some evidence consistent with the idea that scalar adjectives are more likely used as sources than nonscalar ones. As the sight vocabulary features many nonscalar color terms, this helps explains why other than when combined with sound, sight does not commonly feature as a source in linguistic synesthesias. These studies clearly show that language-internal explanations need to be considered alongside language-external ones (cf. Fishman, 2022).

In this study, we argue that before even beginning to discuss what explains the hierarchy of the senses, we need to revisit the available evidence base and ascertain whether the observational data actually lines up with common formulations of the hierarchy; that is, do the available data patterns follow what the hierarchy predicts? Most studies have essentially reapplied the conceptual mold of the hierarchy that was already present in Ullmann to more and more datasets. The predominant perspective has been one of seeking to confirm the hierarchy of the senses. With this comes a particular vantage point from which the data is seen: the existence of a hierarchy of the senses (be it cultural, cognitive, or linguistic in nature, depending on the explanatory approach) is usually *assumed*, and empirical studies are aimed at assessing the degree to which observational and experimental data conform to it. Thanks to a history that spans nearly a century of data collection efforts, we can use the existing data to revisit this vantage point and explore the extent to which different analytical techniques yield different insights.

Starting with Ullmann, scholars working on linguistic synesthesia have published their results in such a way that the summary data can be easily extracted from publications (see Section 3). Moreover, since data presentation generally follows Ullmann's original work quite closely, the data structures that can be extracted from published studies are highly comparable. As a result of this, we are now in the opportune position to conduct the first ever meta-analysis in this field of study, the statistical combination of results from different studies. The time is ripe to take stock of the available evidence and combine data sources for more general inferences on the nature of linguistic synesthesia. This has potentially profound influences for theory development in this space, as the accumulation of evidence allows us to characterize the empirical foundation that motivates theories of linguistic synesthesia in a more precise manner.

Our analyses probe the extant data using a range of analytical techniques that differ with respect to how much they take the hierarchy of the senses as given. In our analyses, we slowly move from a "top-down" perspective of the data towards more bottom-up approaches that make no assumptions about whether there is a hierarchy of the senses prior to seeing the data. By looking at the same data with different analytical approaches, we can, for the first time, assess how the hierarchy of the senses might or might not emerge under different methodological choices, thus also demonstrating how these choices directly impact theory building. Our study is thus concerned with the explanandum, the thing to be explained, and not the explanans, the explanation itself. As we first need to capture a phenomenon before seeking to explain it, the question we address here is arguably more fundamental than the explanatory question and directly impacts it. We ask: What is actually in the data that we seek to explain?

2 Why a Meta-Analysis of Linguistic Synesthesia Is Needed

There are many benefits of combining datasets into a meta-analysis (for general discussion, see Gurevitch et al., 2018; Schmidt, 1992). First, the hierarchy is often presumed to be cross-linguistically universal, or near-universal (e.g., Shen & Gil, 2008; Ullmann, 1959; Williams, 1976); however, individual studies generally focus on only one language at a time, or at most a handful of languages. By combining datasets from different languages, we move research on linguistic synesthesia a small step closer to linguistic typology, where claims about universals are generally based on samples of dozens, often even hundreds of languages (see, e.g., Dryer, 1992; Johansson et al., 2019; Koptjevskaja-Tamm et al., 2024; Urban, 2011; Winter et al., 2022; Youn et al., 2016). In stark contrast to the principles of linguistic typology, the literature on linguistic synesthesia has often been quick to claim universality on the basis of a couple of languages. For example, Williams (1976) spoke of universals against the backdrop of an analysis focused on just English and Japanese; Popova (2005) says that Shen's (1997) extension of linguistic synesthesia research to Hebrew has confirmed the "universal character" of the directionality of mappings (p. 398); Shen and Gil (2008) consider the case for the universal nature of the hierarchy of the senses to be "substantially boosted" if Indonesian would also show the same tendencies (p. 6). Throughout all this research on linguistic synesthesia, we never find that different languages are combined into the same statistical model to assess cross-linguistic generalizability in a formal fashion.

In quantitative linguistic typology, on the other hand, it is common practice to create statistical models aimed at making inferences that go beyond individual languages. This is done by combining data from many different languages into a single dataset (see, e.g., Bickel, 2011; Dryer, 1992), and more specifically, to statistically factor out variation that is due to dependencies between languages emerging from genealogical relatedness and language contact (Bickel, 2015; Cysouw, 2010; Jaeger et al., 2011; Winter & Grice, 2021). If, for example, many different languages from the same language family show a particular asymmetry in linguistic synesthesia, such as touch→sound or taste→smell, this asymmetry could have emerged only once in the ancestral language, which would paint a substantially less universal picture than if the same asymmetry is found again and again across languages from different families. Thus, without formally addressing these dependencies, such as whether languages are genealogically related, claims of universality stand on uncertain grounds (Dunn et al., 2011; Roberts et al., 2015; Roberts & Winters, 2013). The meta-analytic dataset we discuss below, although clearly falling short of the balanced samples that commonly feature in typological studies, is the so-far largest cross-linguistic analysis of linguistic synesthesia, involving 38 datasets from 14 languages, including English, Hungarian, Romanian, French, Italian, German, Korean, Japanese, Spanish, Ancient Greek, Chinese, Latin, Turkish, and Tzotzil. This allows us to put claims of universality to a stronger test than was possible in any one of the individual studies this data comes from.

With respect to amplifying cross-linguistic generalizability, a meta-analysis also provides the opportunity to resolve between "seemingly contradictory research outcomes" (Gurevitch et al., 2018, p. 175), in this case, with respect to studies focused on different languages. For example, Yu (2003, p. 22) observed that his Chinese data "by chance or not, shows no evidence of sight being a less frequent destination than sound," thus apparently contradicting Ullmann's third generalization cited above. It is, however, a common misconception that if a result is found in study A and not in study B, we can logically conclude that the two studies produced different results (cf. "misconception 3" in Vasishth & Nicenboim, 2016, pp. 354–355). Instead, the results from both studies need to be combined to formally test for a difference. The meta-analytic literature is replete with examples where conclusions change when evidence is accumulated across studies; for example, a meta-analysis can reveal effects that are absent when looking at any one study in isolation (e.g., Garg et al., 2008). So, to truly know whether Yu's remarks on Chinese being exceptional are valid, data from Chinese would have to be combined with data from other languages to statistically assess the difference between languages.[3]

A second advantage of performing a meta-analysis is increased statistical power, that is, one's ability to detect statistically reliable patterns, or in the context of a Bayesian analysis, increased precision with which an effect is captured. Both statistical power and precision are greatly affected by how many data points are available for statistical inference, and all else being equal, it is desirable to have more power/precision, which means that it is generally desirable to have more rather than fewer data points. In some specific cases, theoretical claims about the nature of linguistic synesthesia hinge directly on dataset size, as we discuss in Section 3.4 below.

A third advantage of performing a meta-analysis is that analytical approaches vary across studies on linguistic synesthesia, with different studies reporting different measures that are not always comparable (Winter, 2019a, pp. 214–216). For example, several studies have relied on a measure that reports the average percentage of cases that are deemed congruent with the hierarchy of the senses; for example, Shen (1997) reported 95% for Hebrew, Winter (2019a) reported 86% for English, Jo (2019) reported 85% for Korean, Kumcu (2021) reported 95% for Turkish, and Strik-Lievers (2015) reported 62% for English and 74% for Italian. As discussed in Winter (2019a, pp. 214–215), these figures, however, are hard to compare because different studies treat different intersense transfers as congruent with the hierarchy, depending on what specific theoretical model is taken as a baseline. Kumcu (2021) explicitly demonstrates this for his Turkish data, where the number of hierarchy-congruent cases varies from 68% to 95% depending on different interpretations of the hierarchy. A meta-analysis allows us to streamline such analyses to arrive at more consistent results by applying the same analytical methods to all datasets, thus facilitating comparisons across studies, and across languages.

Finally, a meta-analysis offers an opportunity to look at old data with fresh eyes (for an example, see Winter, 2022). Our methodological approach detailed below

---

[3] In fairness to Yu (2003), he did not actually analyze his Chinese data statistically. This, however, makes it even harder to assess whether the data patterns he highlights are truly exceptional. While qualitative research clearly has an important role to play in research on linguistic synesthesia, claims about the hierarchy of the senses can only be addressed statistically because hierarchical tendencies are inherently statistical generalizations. Ullmann himself stressed the statistical nature of his generalizations (Ullmann, 1959, p. 276).

is unique in that we look at the data from different perspectives, thus demonstrating how theoretical conclusions vary as a function of analytical approaches. This allows us to assess the robustness of existing methods: we can, for instance, assess the extent to which studies that previously proclaimed support for the hierarchy may have been unduly influenced by a small number of specific intersense transfers. For example, already Ullmann (1959, p. 284) noted that touch→sound was strikingly over-represented in his data (see also Day, 1996), so much in fact that he briefly considered adding a generalization specifically for this mapping. If our meta-analysis were to find that a small subset of intersense transfers is driving the overall percentage of hierarchy-congruent cases, such as touch→sound, this has the potential to cast serious doubt on the proposal that the hierarchy is a monolithic tendency characterizing all senses in one go. Throughout this study, we will argue that researchers in this field have perhaps not paid enough attention to the contribution of specific mappings and how such specific mappings would impact theorizing in this space. With this, we shift perspective to a more network-based representation of intersense connections, in line with analogous developments in the typology of perception verbs, where the results of large-scale data analyses have moved researchers away from unidimensional hierarchies to more network-oriented representations (e.g., Norcliffe & Majid, 2024). Thus, we want to step out of the cycle of continuously reconfirming the hierarchy using only a subset of the available analytical techniques.

In our meta-analysis, we focus on observational rather than experimental studies for the following reasons: first, observational studies arguably make up the majority of studies, and serve as the starting point for all experimental research on linguistic synesthesia, many of which are aimed at explaining the patterns seen in the corpus or dictionary data. Second, experimental tasks in this literature are too variegated, with a diverse range of tasks and response measures used to address a diverse set of research questions. This makes it hard to meaningfully combine existing experimental studies into a meta-analysis. If one experimental study collected naturalness ratings for different linguistic synesthesias, for example, this is hard to compare to another study where participants were asked to give comprehension judgments, especially if the participant populations and the stimulus characteristics also vary across studies.

We proceed as follows. Section 3 uses an example dataset to illustrate the type of data that is the input to our meta-analysis. In this section, we focus on the connection between methods and theory, and how in the study of linguistic synesthesia, just as in other domains of linguistic inquiry, all theoretical conclusions are contingent on one's analytical approach. Section 4 introduces the methods of our meta-analysis. Sections 5–8 present our results, which involves four different analyses, each with its own perspective on the network of intersense connections. Section 9 provides an in-depth discussion of what we can conclude from our analysis and how our data changes the very nature of the research questions we can ask in this field of study. Most importantly, we propose that our analyses shift the explanandum, which in turn directly affects what explanatory approaches are viable or not. If, for example, most patterns in linguistic synesthesia data would turn out not to fit the hierarchy of the senses, the hierarchy would also not be needed as an explanatory construct.

3 The Hierarchy of the Senses: Evidence and Theory

3.1 An Example Dataset

In this section, we introduce the type of data analyzed in our meta-analysis. Given that it formed the basis of all subsequent work on linguistic synesthesia, Stephen Ullmann's work must be our point of reference. When studying linguistic synesthesias, Ullmann was chiefly concerned with poetic language use. He collated linguistic synesthesias from French, Hungarian, and English poets and presented tables such as Table 1, which shows data from Lord Byron's writings (Ullmann, 1945, p. 814). The rows in Table 1 represent the sources; columns correspond to targets. The values in the cells represent token counts of specific source-target combinations; for example, the touch row/sound column cell lists 76 tokens, which means that Ullmann was able to collate this many expressions in Lord Byron's writings where the source is related to touch, and the target is related to sound. Expressions such as *smooth melody* or *rough sound* would be included in the counts of this specific cell.

Tables such as this one abound in the literature on linguistic synesthesia, including in the decades following Ullmann's initial work (e.g., Mancaș, 1962; Rosiello, 1963; Whitney, 1952), all the way up to modern studies (Jo, 2019; Kumcu, 2021; Strik-Lievers, 2015; Winter, 2019a; Zhao et al., 2019). The availability of similarly structured data is what makes our meta-analysis possible. Data can only be meaningfully combined if they are actually comparable across studies. There are, however, important differences between studies that need to be highlighted: firstly, across datasets and within individual datasets, different studies focus on different kinds of linguistic expressions. Secondly, researchers have compiled their datasets using different sources and methods. These dimensions of variation are elaborated upon in Sections 3.2 and 3.3 below.

3.2 Types of Linguistic Synesthesia Represented in Published Datasets

A distinction can be drawn between instances of conventional and novel synesthesia (Strik-Lievers, 2016). Conventional linguistic synesthesias

Table 1 Counts of linguistic synesthesias broken up by sources (rows) and targets (columns), based on an analysis of Lord Byron's writings from Ullmann (1945, p. 814)

	Touch	Heat	Taste	Smell	Sound	Sight	Total
Touch	(-)	8	3	3	76	31	121
Heat	2	(-)	2	-	11	9	24
Taste	1	-	(-)	1	7	8	17
Smell	-	-	-	(-)	3	2	5
Sound	-	-	-	-	(-)	11	11
Sight	5	3	-	1	21	(-)	30
	8	11	5	5	118	61	208

found in everyday language involve the adaptation of the source expression's meaning to that of the target expression. In *sweet melody*, for example, *sweet*'s reference to the domain of taste is backgrounded, while the more general evaluative meaning, which is compatible with *melody*, is retained; the auditory use of *sweet* is usually also acknowledged by dictionaries; for example, the Oxford English Dictionary entry for *sweet* has 'pleasing to the ear' alongside 'pleasing to the sense of taste'. As Prandi (2023, p. 25) notes, at the lexical level, "conventional metaphors surface as extended senses of polysemous words." On the other hand, in novel linguistic synesthesias, typically found in poetry, the meaning of the source is not adapted to that of the target. For example, in Italian *voci di tenebra azzurra* 'voices of light blue darkness' (Giovanni Pascoli, *La mia sera*), the meaning of what is arguably the source expression, *tenebra azzurra*, 'light blue darkness', maintains its visual meaning, which clashes with the auditory meaning of *voci* 'voices'. The reader has to interpret this conceptual clash, and no dictionary lists an auditory meaning for *tenebra* 'darkness'. Regarding generalizations about preferences in the combination of sensory modalities, it may be hypothesized that conventional linguistic synesthesias exhibit a greater degree of conformity to such preferences compared to novel ones. Although no systematic study on this specific issue is available, it can be expected that novel synesthesias, arising from the creative endeavors of their authors, may encompass a broader range of sensory pairings, including perhaps a higher proportion of "counter-directional" ones that go against the hierarchy.

Datasets vary in the relative prevalence of novel or conventional synesthesias. Although most studies do not provide a complete list of the linguistic synesthesias their tables are based on, datasets based solely on literary texts, whether prose or poetry, can arguably be expected to feature a higher number of novel synesthetic expressions compared to datasets derived from general language texts. Dictionaries, on the other hand, try to capture general language use and can therefore be expected to mostly consist of conventional synesthetic expressions (see Section 3.3). Indeed, the frequency with which a particular sensory word is used in the context of another sensory modality, such as *sweet* repeatedly being applied to describe sounds, is what drives lexicographers to propose that there is polysemy, thus warranting a subentry.

Additionally, datasets differ in which syntactic manifestations of linguistic synesthesias they consider (for a discussion of syntactic aspects of synesthesias in different languages, see Catricalà, 2008; De Salazar, 2019; Dombi, 1974; Marotta, 2011; Rosiello, 1963). Adjective-noun pairs like English *smooth melody, sweet fragrance*, and *loud color* are the most commonly studied manifestation of linguistic synesthesia (e.g., Day, 1996; Kumcu, 2021; Strik-Lievers, 2015; Ullmann, 1959; Winter, 2019a; Zhao et al., 2019). Already Ullmann (1959, p. 278) suggested that adjective-noun pairs dominate linguistic synesthesia, and this conjecture has since then been supported by quantitative data from Strik-Lievers and Huang (2016), who show that adjective-noun pairs actually dominate in linguistic synesthesia (Marotta, 2011, explores what motivates this prevalence). In other linguistic constructions, cross-sensory conflict is generated by the syntactic connection of, for instance, verb and direct object (1), verb and subject (2), verb and adverbial predicate (3), noun and adjectival predicate (4), or noun and genitive (5).

(1) Spanish, from Pérez Galdós, *El Empecinado* (Doetsch Kraus, 1992, p. 75)
    Estoy pintando el silencio
    'I am painting silence'
(2) English, from George Herbert, *Christmas* (Ullmann, 1959, p. 271)
    Till ev'n his beams sing, and my musick shine
(3) German, from Patrick Süskind, *Das Parfum* (Strik-Lievers, 2016, p. 55)
    Grenouille sah den ganzen Markt riechend
    'Grenouille saw the whole market smelling'
(4) Italian (Catricalà, 2008, p. 48)
    I colori sono chiassosi
    'Colors are loud'
(5) Latin, from Cicero, *Brutus* (Ullmann, 1959, p. 268)
    Splendor vocis
    'Splendor of voice'

Linguistic synesthesia is also found at the lexical level, in compound words such as Korean 단내 *ta-n-nay* 'sweet smell' from Jo (2018, p. 41). Finally, in a logographic language like Chinese, individual characters referring to a modality but with a radical from a different modality may be considered a case of "sublexical synesthesia," as argued by Huang and Xiong (2019, p. 295). For example, the Chinese character 聞 *wén* 'to smell' contains the radical 耳 *ěr* 'ear' that is related to audition.

Certain datasets exclusively feature linguistic synesthesias of a single structure, most commonly adjective-noun pairs (Kumcu, 2021; Paissa, 1995; Salzmann, 2014; Winter, 2019a; Zhao et al., 2019). Only few studies focus on synesthesias in other forms, such as genitive phrases (Shen & Gadir, 2009) and compounds (Jo, 2018). Other studies do not specify whether they concentrate on particular structures or explicitly state that they include a variety of structures in their datasets (Doetsch Kraus, 1992; Fujimoto, 2001; Strik-Lievers, 2015; Ullmann, 1959; Whitney, 1952).

3.3 Data Sources and Methods Used to Create Datasets

Two primary sources of data feature in observational studies of linguistic synesthesias: text corpora and, less commonly, dictionaries. As mentioned in Section 3.2, dictionary-based studies (Catricalà, 2008; Jo, 2018; Paissa, 1995; Salzmann, 2014) focus on the lexicalized, conventional synesthetic expressions that are recorded in the (polysemous) lexical entries of sensory lexemes. Paissa (1995) explains that for her dictionary-based study of French and Italian synesthesia, she first compiled a list of all adjectives that can refer to a specific sensory modality, based on dictionary definitions. She then examined each adjective to determine whether it could combine with nouns from a different sensory modality, relying on adjective-noun phrases found in the examples provided in the lexical entries. For instance, the Italian adjective *acuto* 'sharp' has touch as its primary sense, but in the dictionaries consulted, it is also used to modify such nouns as *vista* 'sight,' *suono* 'sound,' and *odore* 'smell.' Thus, *acuto* adds +1 to the cells corresponding to touch→sight, touch→sound, and touch→smell transfers. In a way, dictionary studies represent a subset of the types of linguistic synesthesias present in corpora, the latter being likely to also contain a higher frequency of relatively more creative, novel linguistic synesthesias that may be too rare to be recorded in dictionaries. On the other hand, dictionaries might include linguistic synesthesias that are not attested in corpora of the same language, as their absence in corpora does not necessarily entail that they are absent in the language.

Corpus studies of linguistic synesthesia involve different text types. Some studies restrict their focus to literary texts, including prose, poetry, or both. Ullmann (1959) focused on literary data and justified this focus by stating that this would be likely to yield more linguistic synesthesias and therefore afford stronger quantitative generalizations: "Ordinary language contains a certain number of synaesthetic transfers, but not enough for our purpose" (p. 276). In other studies, the aim is to describe the sensory combinations used by specific authors, therefore restricting corpora to the works of these authors (e.g., Ullmann, 1947, on Théophile Gautier; Whitney, 1952 on seven Hungarian poets from the twentieth century; Rosiello, 1963 on Eugenio Montale; Day, 1996 on Thomas Mann's *Buddenbrooks*). While most earlier works have focused on literary texts, the more recent availability of large reference corpora, such as the Corpus of Contemporary American English (Winter, 2019a) and the Sinica corpus for Chinese (Zhao et al., 2019), has enabled researchers to study linguistic synesthesia in general language use (see also Jo, 2017, 2022; Kumcu, 2021; Strik-Lievers, 2015). Other studies look at specialized corpora, such as Zawisławska (2019), who analyzed linguistic synesthesia in a corpus of sensory-related blog posts, including culinary blogs posts and reviews of beer, coffee, and perfumes.

Corpus studies differ not only in the type of texts they include but also in the methods they use to identify instances of synesthesia. In early studies such as Ullmann's, researchers had no alternative but to meticulously read through texts, identify synesthetic expressions, and manually annotate the source and target sensory modalities to create tables such as Table 1. This is a time-consuming procedure which often leads to relatively small datasets of carefully selected and analyzed linguistic synesthesias. Importantly, this approach does not guarantee that any researcher reading the same texts would identify the same linguistic synesthesias and annotate them in the same way: metaphor identification and annotation is a notoriously complex task, partly influenced by the researcher's theoretical convictions, as well as by their personal interpretation of a text. This limits the reproducibility of research on linguistic synesthesia (Winter, 2019a, Ch. 10.4.1).

In more recent studies based on large electronic corpora, the identification and annotation of linguistic synesthesias have been partially or fully automated. In Strik-Lievers (2015), candidate instances of synesthesia are automatically extracted from corpus data using pre-established lists of nouns, verbs, and adjectives for each sensory modality, and are then manually checked. Many other scholars have adopted similar procedures (Jo, 2017, 2022; Kumcu, 2021; Zhao et al., 2019). Winter (2019a) assumes a continuous notion of sensory modalities, using norming data where words are rated for the strength of their association with each sensory modality (Lynott & Connell, 2009). After selecting words that refer relatively exclusively to a single modality (e.g., *yellow*, rated very high for sight and very low for the other modalities), all cross-sensory adjective-noun pairs are automatically extracted from a large corpus, without subsequent manual checking. While datasets derived from partially automatic extraction procedures are more "controlled" – though sharing with manually built datasets a degree of dependence on researchers' choices and interpretations – fully automatic procedures are more likely to include "noise," such as false positives, that is, expressions that are included in data analysis that may not actually be instances of linguistic synesthesia. For example, the English expression *bright voice* might be included in a fully automated analysis because *bright* is primarily visual and *voice* is primarily auditory, even though in context, the expression could have been used not to describe an auditory impression, but the speaker's intelligence. Werning et al. (2006) discuss the latter case as "weak linguistic synesthesia," where only the source is perceptual, in contrast to "strong linguistic synesthesia," where both the source and the target are perceptual. When *bright voice* is included in the sight→sound cell due to using a fully automated analysis that does not take context into account, this would be an instance of a false positive entering the analysis.

It should be emphasized that all these methods, whether manual or automatic, necessarily assume a particular approach to sensory categorization. There are, in fact, two assumptions that go into any analysis that generates outputs such as Table 1 discussed above. The first assumption relates to how the sensorium is divided into separate senses, and in fact, even more fundamentally, *whether* the sensorium can be divided into separate senses to begin with (Winter, 2019a, Ch. 2). Extensive debates have taken place since antiquity, and across multiple disciplines, regarding how many and what senses there are, and whether they can be clearly separated into distinct categories. Perceptual psychologists, for example, have considered whether taste and smell can actually be separated given their abundant behavioral and neural integration (see, e.g., Auvray & Spence, 2008). Similarly, what we call "touch" in English and many other languages is actually composed of a conglomerate of different receptors and neural subsystems that respond separately to pressure, vibration, temperature, or pain (Carlson, 2010). Studies on linguistic synesthesia differ in how the senses are categorized. For example, some studies separate touch from temperature (Bretones-Callejas, 2001; Day, 1996; Ronga et al., 2012; Ullmann, 1959), while others do not (Kumcu, 2021; Strik-Lievers, 2015; Winter, 2019a; Zhao et al., 2019). The majority of studies, however, use the five senses folk model that we have inherited from antiquity via Aristoteles, namely, a separation of the senses into sight, sound, touch, taste, and smell. Given its dominance in this field of inquiry, we will also adopt this model.

Once a theoretical decision has been made with respect to what number of senses to assume as a baseline, a second set of assumptions comes in when categorizing sensory words with respect to these sensory modalities. Given that many sensory words are multisensory (Lynott & Connell, 2009), different researchers may classify the same sensory word differently (Ronga, 2016; Winter, 2019a, Ch. 10), either based on their own intuitive judgments or based on different methodologies used for classification. For example, Strik-Lievers and Huang (2016) used corpora, WordNet, and other lexical resources to derive their word list, and Winter (2019a) used data from a rating study where words were rated for their association with different sensory modalities on a continuous scale (Lynott & Connell, 2009). In dictionary-based studies that explicitly address the methodological concern of how words are classified according to the senses (Paissa 1995), the primary sensory modality of polysensory lexical items is determined through a combination of researcher judgment, etymology (with the primary modality being the one referenced in the earliest recorded usage), and the order of appearance in the dictionary entry (with the first listed sense considered primary). Altogether, however, the majority of studies do not comment on the methodological issue of classifying sensory words, and it can be assumed that for most of these studies, researchers used their own intuitive judgments.

Despite the diversity in data and methods, researchers have identified recurring patterns in the way the senses tend to be associated with each other in linguistic synesthesia, as discussed in Section 1. In our meta-analysis, our primary goal is to use the combination of all available datasets to reassess which generalizations the data actually support. To the extent that studies vary in their methodology (e.g., whether manual or automatic extraction was used, or how the sensory vocabulary was classified), obtaining patterns that are consistent across studies can be assumed to be highly generalizable; that is, these patterns are obtained *despite* methodological variation. When particular methodological choices are consistently reported and there are enough studies to allow comparison between choices, a meta-analysis allows us to directly investigate the impact of methodological variation. Here, we will assess to what extent data type (corpus versus dictionary) and genre (general versus literary) impact results. It will not be possible to directly test how generalizations are impacted by the distinction between novel and conventional synesthesia as datasets are more mixed in this respect; that is, both are usually included in the same cell count, without separating the data so that we would be able to analyze it. What exactly counts as conventional or novel is also a matter of degree, and definitions of novelty or conventionality vary across studies. However, if an impact of data type and genre was detected, this could be interpreted as an indirect indicator – to be further verified with targeted studies – of a difference between conventional and novel synesthesias in terms of preferred patterns of sensory combinations. This is because, as mentioned above, literary language and, to some extent, corpus studies can be presumed to contain a slightly higher proportion of novel synesthesias compared to general language and dictionary studies.

A final relevant aspect of variation in datasets is the overall size of the dataset, ranging from as little as 15 linguistic synesthesias observed for Tzotzil by Catricalà (2008) to 8,082 observed for Chinese by Zhao et al. (2019). In the following section, we highlight a particular theoretical issue that is directly impacted by data set size.

3.4 Unidirectionality versus Asymmetry

Metaphor research distinguishes between asymmetry and unidirectionality (Boroditsky, 2000; Winter et al., 2015). Unidirectionality involves metaphorical transfers that move in one direction (A→B) in an exceptionless manner; that is, the reverse mapping (B→A) is never attested in a corpus. Asymmetry, on the other hand, involves bidirectional connections, but they are biased; for example, A→B is more frequent than B→A. Zhao et al. (2019) call asymmetric mappings in linguistic synesthesia "biased-directional." They classify linguistic synesthesias in Chinese as unidirectional or biased-directional (here: asymmetric) based on whether a reverse transfer is or is not attested in the Sinica Corpus.

The asymmetry of metaphorical mappings is a core tenet of conceptual metaphor theory that has received empirical backing by both experimental studies (e.g., Boroditsky, 2000; Bottini & Casasanto, 2013; Casasanto & Boroditsky, 2008), as well as typological research (Urban, 2011; Winter & Srinivasan, 2021). However, in contrast to asymmetry, unidirectionality may be too strict of a criterion. For example, while English speakers frequently talk about time in terms of spatial language, such as saying *Christmas is coming* or *The meeting is two days ahead of us*, it is possible, but presumed to be less common, to talk about space using time, such as when saying *We are twenty minutes away from Birmingham* (Casasanto & Boroditsky, 2008, pp. 589–590). Thus, SPACE IS TIME metaphors exhibit asymmetry (space is used more often to talk about time than the reverse) and not unidirectionality (time is never used to talk about space).

Consider how the sight→taste cell in Table 1 from Ullmann's analysis of Lord Byron's writing is empty, whereas there are 8 cases in the taste→sight cell. Following Zhao et al.'s (2019) logic, we would conclude that taste→sight is a unidirectional rather than asymmetric ("biased-directional") mapping for this dataset because no counterexample exists in this specific corpus. If, however, we found just a single additional instance for the sight→taste cell, the relationship between sight and taste would be demoted to being merely asymmetric, rather than unidirectional. This highlights that claims of unidirectionality are extremely dependent on sample size, which suggests that unidirectionality in corpus research is too flimsy a notion, easily falsified by a single counterexample. Just like research on conceptual metaphors, most research on linguistic synesthesia has moved beyond concerns of unidirectionality, having firmly established that asymmetry is the norm (Strik-Lievers, 2015). Already Ullmann (1959) emphasized the statistical nature of the tendencies observed (p. 275), noting that there will always tend to be exceptions, with different reverse mappings being attested for different authors.

Since Ullmann's original set of analyses, many of the cells for reverse mappings that he found to be empty have been filled in other studies (e.g., Day, 1996; Shen, 1997), which led Winter (2019a, p. 10) to say: "Given the already established evidence, it must be the case that the hierarchy of the senses is about metaphorical asymmetry rather than unidirectionality." Our meta-analysis features more data than any previous analysis of linguistic synesthesia, which allows us to finally put the nail on the coffin of the unidirectionality versus asymmetry issue, showing that it does, in fact, entirely depend on data size. The theoretical shift from unidirectionality towards asymmetry, however, has important ramifications for both analytical methods and theoretical conceptions of linguistic synesthesia: for asymmetrical mappings, we have to actively consider *the degree* to which a given pair of modalities is biased towards sources or targets, rather than focusing on *whether* a particular sense features as a source or as a target.

3.5 Frequency, Asymmetry, and Ambiguity about the Hierarchy

In the literature on linguistic synesthesia, researchers often make statements such as the following: "synesthetic metaphor transfers at large go from the 'lower' to the 'higher' sensory modes" (Jo, 2018, p. 38), or, "we suggest that mapping goes from lower modalities onto higher ones" (Shen & Cohen, 1998, p. 123). Such statements echo Ullmann, who, as mentioned above, proposed that intersensory transfers "tend to mount from the lower to the higher reaches of the sensorium, from the less differentiated sensations to the more differentiated ones, and not *vice versa*" (Ullmann, 1959, p. 280). In this section, we want to point out that these rather coarse verbal statements are actually compatible with a number of different data patterns, and researchers in this literature have not always been particularly clear about what precise data patterns are specifically targeted by theoretical proposals.

First, these verbal statements are couched in a binary divide between the lower and the higher senses, even though the hierarchy is generally interpreted in terms of a linear cline, as in Viberg's (1983) model. Verbal statements that reference lower-to-higher mappings leave open the question of whether relative differences *between* the lower modalities are treated as important or not, and the same applies to differences between the higher modalities of sound and sight. In other words: do we treat the presumed-to-be lower senses of touch, taste, and smell as equals, or do we assume that some of them are "lower" or "higher" with respect to each other? And the same goes for the relative positioning of sound vis-à-vis sight among the "higher" modalities – does it matter?

Visual depictions of the hierarchy generally feature taste on a lower position than smell, in which case taste→smell mappings (e.g., *sour scent*) could be treated as hierarchy-congruent, but the above statements would not capture such a relation if only mappings from lower to higher senses are treated as hierarchy-congruent. The same goes for sight→sound (e.g., *luminous pitch*), a relation between the two higher modalities that Ullmann (1959) already noted to be very common. If this mapping is indeed so frequent, then clearly the lower-to-higher characterization of the hierarchy would not capture all data patterns, unless we are willing to put sound, the most common target of transfers, as "higher" than sight. If we were to do this, however, we would change our understanding of what modalities are treated as lower or higher on the basis of having seen the data, rather than on the basis of a hierarchy that is independently motivated by factors external to the data. In that case, we could not claim that the pre-established notion of "lower" and "higher" senses predicts patterns in the data. To flesh out proposals of the hierarchy of the senses, researchers have to be more explicit about whether or not there are relative differences between the lower and higher senses, which would also require specifying exactly how taste is "lower" than smell, or how sight is "lower" than sound. Unfortunately, we never find detailed theoretical proposals on these important points.

A second major ambiguity hidden in theoretical claims such as the above statements relates to the contrast between frequency and asymmetry. As discussed in Section 3.4, we take asymmetry to be the extent to which for two bidirectionally connected senses, A→B is more frequent than B→A. Thus described, asymmetry relates to the *relative* frequency of A→B versus B→A, which we quantify in terms of source/target ratios below. For example, in Table 1 above, touch→sight occurs 31 times, compared to sight→touch, which occurs only 5 times. This yields a source/target ratio of 6.2, indicating a high degree of pairwise asymmetry: touch→sight is about 6 times more frequent than the reverse mapping. In using ratios, this statement completely ignores the *absolute* frequency of the pairing, however. The same ratio of 6.2 would also result from comparing 3,100 cases of touch→sight to 500 cases of sight→touch. While the pairwise asymmetry is left unchanged (the ratio is 6.2 in both cases), the second example clearly captures a larger number of linguistic synesthesias. When it comes to characterizing what patterns dominate the data, absolute frequency therefore needs to be considered alongside pairwise asymmetry. Verbal statements characterizing mappings as going from "lower" to "higher" senses generally gloss over the asymmetry versus absolute frequency distinction.

Thus, common verbal descriptions of the hierarchy leave many questions unanswered: How do we deal with variation between the lower senses, and variation between the higher senses? And are lower-to-higher mappings presumed to be only about asymmetry, or do they also cover absolute frequency? Both of these questions actually relate to a third, open question: How do we deal with situations where specific pairings are greatly over- or under-represented? This is a key issue of theoretical concern because it is possible that the majority of the "lower-to-higher" mappings are driven by one or a handful of *specific* mappings, for example, touch→sound. Can we really speak of a hierarchy as a monolithic concept if one of the lower-to-higher mappings is greatly more frequent than the others? And related to this, what do we do if the mapping between the two "higher" senses, sight→sound, may actually turn out to be *more* frequent than many of the lower-to-higher mappings? We will argue that the literature on linguistic synesthesia has, so far, not paid enough attention to particular pairings of senses, that is, specific mappings. Without directly and explicitly addressing the over-representation of specific mappings, it is not clear at all whether a monolithic hierarchy is actually a sensible theoretical construct for the observed data patterns. Our meta-analysis will directly tackle some of the questions that have been missed in research on linguistic synesthesia, and in doing so, we point to important dimensions along which theoretical proposals about the hierarchy are underspecified.

4 Methods

4.1 Datasets Included in the Analyses

All our analyses are of linguistic synesthesia tables such as the one shown in Table 1, including a total of 28 comparable tables of linguistic synesthesia from corpus data, and 10 similarly structured tables coming from dictionary data. Table 2 shows the full list of corpus datasets that are included in our meta-analysis. Table 3 shows the full list of dictionary datasets we considered. Fujimoto (2001) includes a mixture of both but is predominantly dictionary, and our results reported below do not differ regardless of whether it is classified as corpus or dictionary.

Table 2 Corpus datasets included in our analyses; lit. = literary language; gen. = general language; total N refers to the total number of linguistic synesthesias, summed across all cells of each table

Reference	Language	Type	Total N	Data source
Bretones-Callejas (2001)	English	lit.	33	writings of S. Heaney
Day (1996)	English	lit.	1269	various
Day (1996)	German	lit.	177	T. Mann's *Buddenbrooks*
Doetsch Kraus (1992)	Spanish	lit.	2419	various
Jo (2017)	Korean	gen.	100	Korean National Corpus
Jo (2022)	Korean	gen.	315	Sejong corpus
Kumcu (2021)	Turkish	gen.	5693	Turkish National Corpus
Mancaş (1962)	Romanian	lit.	102	writings of T. Arghezi
Mancaş (1962)	Romanian	lit.	119	writings of M. Eminescu (in vita)
Mancaş (1962)	Romanian	lit.	231	writings of M. Eminescu (posthumous)
Mancaş (1962)	Romanian	lit.	429	writings of M. Sadoveanu
Rosiello (1963)	Italian	lit.	99	writings of E. Montale
Strik-Lievers (2015)	English	gen.	500	ukWaC corpus
Strik-Lievers (2015)	Italian	gen.	500	itkWaC corpus
Ullmann (1937)	English	lit.	302	writings of W. Morris
Ullmann (1945)	English	lit.	217	writings of Lord Byron
Ullmann (1945)	English	lit.	173	writings of J. Keats
Ullmann (1946)	French	lit.	164	writings of C. Leconte de Lisle
Ullmann (1947)	French	lit.	233	writings of T. Gautier
Whitney (1952)	Hungarian	lit.	190	writings of E. Ady
Whitney (1952)	Hungarian	lit.	192	writings of M. Babits
Whitney (1952)	Hungarian	lit.	172	writings of G. Illyés
Whitney (1952)	Hungarian	lit.	138	writings of A. József
Whitney (1952)	Hungarian	lit.	173	writings of L. Kassák
Whitney (1952)	Hungarian	lit.	102	writings of D. Kosztolányi
Whitney (1952)	Hungarian	lit.	95	writings of A. Tóth
Winter (2019a)	English	gen.	5880	COCA corpus
Zhao et al. (2019)	Chinese	gen.	8082	Sinica corpus

Table 3 Dictionary datasets included in our analyses; total N refers to the total number of linguistic synesthesias, summed across all cells of each table

Reference	Language	Total N
Catricalà (2008)	Ancient Greek	41
Catricalà (2008)	English	62
Catricalà (2008)	Latin	44
Catricalà (2008)	Spanish	46
Catricalà (2008)	Tzotzil	15
Fujimoto (2001)	Japanese	261
Jo (2018)	Korean	50
Paissa (1995)	French	123
Paissa (1995)	Italian	107
Salzmann (2014)	German	99

For any meta-analysis, it is important to be explicit about which studies were included or excluded. We strive for a dataset that maximizes comparability of data structures as well as diversity of data sources, combining different types of data (corpus and dictionary), genres (general language and literary), and languages. After collating a superset of all potential candidate datasets, some datasets had to be excluded, for a variety of reasons. For instance, Fishman's (2022) English corpus data are intersensory analogies of the form *The picture looks like my music sounds*, which, although clearly related to our topic, are not treated as instances of linguistic synesthesia in our study (see Strik-Lievers, 2018 on the relationship between synesthesia and other non-synesthetic sensory figures). Zawisławska (2019) on Polish is not included because the corpus consists of blog posts on sensory-related topics, mostly food and drink, cosmetics, perfumes: results therefore represent some senses more than others and are hard to compare to the bulk of studies in this field, which generally look at texts that are not focused on specific sensory stimuli. For this reason, we also excluded Sanz-Valdivieso and López-Arroyo's (2024) dataset of linguistic synesthesias in English olive oil tasting notes, and Strik-Lievers' (2015) dataset of linguistic synesthesias in Patrick Süskind's novel *The Perfume*, which features an over-representation of smell. Marotta (2012) and De Felice (2014) analyze the synesthetic usages of sensory adjectives in corpora (Italian and Latin respectively), but they only consider adjectives from a subset of the five senses, which makes their tables not comparable with those of other studies.

Similarly, Ronga et al. (2012) investigate Italian corpus data, but only look at auditory and tactile synesthesias. We had to rule out a single study (Dombi, 1974) that would have met our inclusion criteria but that used percentages that did not allow reconstructing precise frequencies. Zhao et al.'s study (2024) was not considered here because our dataset already included a prior analysis of the same Sinica corpus by the same author team (Zhao et al., 2019).

The 38 datasets included in our analyses are published between 1937 and 2022. The datasets also represent different time periods, from Ancient Greek and Latin to (different stages of) modern languages (Spanish texts analyzed by Doetsch Kraus, 1992, for instance, range from 1440 to 1850). As discussed in Section 3.3, corpus datasets are built based either on literary texts or on large corpora representing general language use. After finding that the genre distinction (literary versus general) did not impact the results in our first analysis reported in Section 5.2, we decided to combine all data in one integrated analysis.

For the corpus data, the question arises as to whether one looks at counts of word types, word tokens, or other measures, such as hapax legomena (Kumcu, 2021; Ronga, 2016; Winter, 2019a, pp. 215–216). It is possible, for example, that the majority of tokens for a specific mapping, say, taste→sound, are driven by the same lexical items, such as, *sweet music*, *sweet sound*, and *sweet melody*. If this were to be the case, characterizing the mapping as being primarily about 'taste' and 'sound' would be off. Studying how conclusions are impacted by considering word tokens versus word types is one way of addressing the lexical productivity of particular mappings. Unfortunately, too few studies report these different types of word counts, which is why we chose to analyze the most used statistic, token counts. We are less concerned about whether the patterns we study below are productive across a large class of lexical items, in part because previous research has shown this to be the case (Kumcu, 2021; Ronga, 2016; Winter, 2019a, pp. 215–216), and in part because we also include dictionary data, which only represents types, not tokens. After finding that the distinction between corpus tokens and dictionary types does not matter in our first analysis below (Section 5.2), we decided to simplify our presentation of the results by including everything in one integrated analysis, the same way that we have done for genre. That said, it is important to keep in mind that throughout our analyses, the token-versus-type distinction is identified with the distinction between corpus data and dictionary data. To the extent that this distinction is not shown to matter, the results reported below are in line with the idea that linguistic synesthesia is lexically productive, although they do not test this idea as directly as would be possible if the raw corpus data was available for all studies.

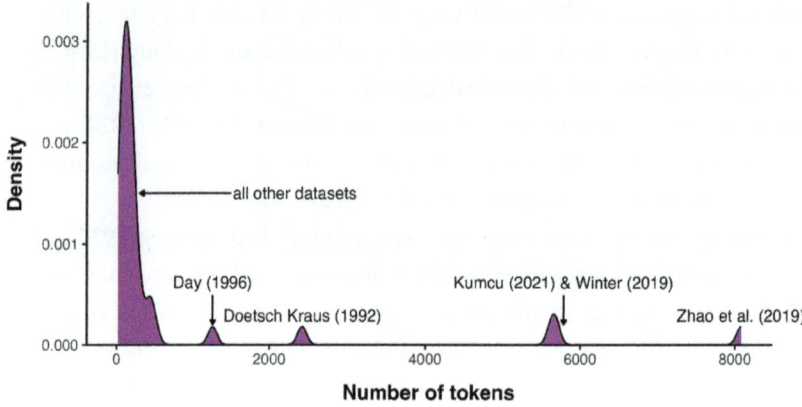

Figure 1 Distribution of token counts across the 38 datasets

The datasets vary greatly in terms of the total number of tokens that they include, ranging from 15 tokens for Tzotzil (Catricalà, 2008) 2001 to 8,082 tokens for Chinese (Zhao et al., 2019). Figure 1 displays the distribution of tokens across studies, which shows that there are a few studies that have very many tokens (e.g., Kumcu, 2021; Winter, 2019a; Zhao et al., 2019), while the majority of studies have less than 1000 tokens, represented by the hill on the left. The average number of tokens is 771; the median is 163. The potentially problematic issue of differing number of data points across studies will be addressed in our analyses in Section 5).

4.2 Cross-Linguistic Diversity

Our dataset features 14 distinct languages from seven different language families (Indo-European: Latin, French, Spanish, Italian, Romanian, English, German, Ancient Greek; Finno-Ugric: Hungarian; Turkic: Turkish; Mayan: Tzotzil; Sino-Tibetan: Chinese; Isolate: Korean, Isolate: Japanese). Figure 2 shows the breakdown of the number of datasets per language, with colors indicating different language families.

We should openly address that while our sample represents a massive step forward in terms of being able to make cross-linguistic generalizations, compared to previous studies, our dataset still constitutes a heavily biased sample. First, 63% of the datasets in this meta-analysis are Indo-European. Second, the dataset features only seven language families in total, whereas it is common in typological research to generalize over multiple dozens of language families. Third, in terms of cross-linguistic diversity, entire continents are absent from this data; for example, there are no languages from Africa or Australia. In fact, some of the largest language families, such as Niger-Congo and Austronesian, are conspicuously absent from

Linguistic Synesthesia

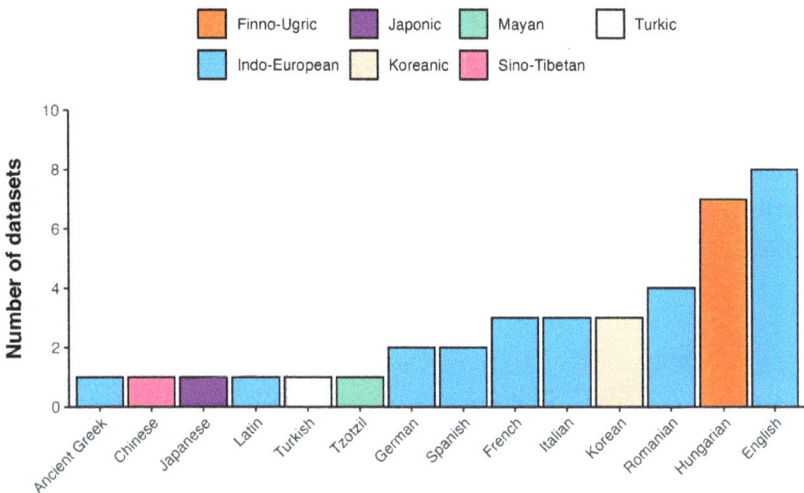

Figure 2 Number of datasets per language; colors indicate language family associations

this sample. Fourth, except for Tzotzil, all languages in the sample come from major world languages with millions of speakers who live in industrialized societies, and even Tzotzil is a comparatively large language. This is an important caveat for drawing strong cross-linguistic generalizations about linguistic synesthesia given that it is known that languages spoken by small hunter-gatherer communities can in some cases have much more extensive smell vocabularies, such as the two Aslian languages Jahai and Maniq spoken in Malaysia and Thailand (Majid & Burenhult, 2014; Wnuk & Majid, 2014). Fifth and finally, our sample does not include data from any signed language. Given that language is both spoken and signed, the currently available evidence does not allow making generalizations about intersensory connections that are independent of linguistic modality. True universals of language require the inclusion of signed languages in typological analysis (see, e.g., Sandler & Lillo-Martin, 2006).

While clearly exposing limitations of our analysis in terms of cross-linguistic generalizability, Figure 2 and our discussion in this section also highlight an additional reason for doing a meta-analysis, in that it draws attention to what has been systematically missed in research on linguistic synesthesia up to this point. It is important to emphasize that past claims to the universality of linguistic synesthesia were decidedly premature, in that entire modalities of linguistic expression (signed languages) have been missed, as well as different sensory cultures, such as those that have been reported for some hunter-gatherer communities. Up to this point, all generalizations about linguistic synesthesia only relate to a restricted subset of languages, namely, those languages that are spoken, and within that, the even smaller subset of languages that are spoken by large populations in industrialized societies, especially Indo-European languages. Finally, we must acknowledge that although we have put a lot of effort into finding all published datasets on linguistic synesthesia, we most certainly will have missed datasets that are published in languages that are not accessible to us.

4.3 Data Merging

Not all data could immediately be entered into analysis without further modification. With few exceptions (Bretones-Callejas, 2001; Day, 1996; Ronga et al., 2012), most studies since Ullmann have given up the distinction between temperature and touch. Since temperature-related linguistic synesthesias such as *warm sound* and *cool color* are subsumed under touch in modern work, we first merged the two categories. Second, we aligned the tables so that all rows and all columns were arranged in the same order. Third, Doetsch Kraus (1992) reports two tables, one each for conventional and creative linguistic synesthesias. As no other studies separated these dimensions, we collapsed the counts of these two tables into one table by summing. Fourth, Day (1996) shows tables that are transposed with respect to all other tables; that is, rows are swapped with columns. It is clear from his discussion that he interpreted his tables in the conventional way, following Ullmann's earlier work. Thus, for the data from Day (1996), we transposed tables. Fifth and finally, only Winter (2019a) reported unimodal cases; that is, the diagonal in Table 1 would be filled with *intra*sense adjective-noun pairs (e.g., *abrasive touch*, *loud sound*). As no other study included these figures, the diagonal of Winter's (2019a) table was excluded. All data exclusion and merging steps are detailed in the Open Science Framework repository associated with this publication: https://osf.io/457yb/

4.4 Software Implementation

We analyzed the data using R version 4.4.0 (R Core Team, 2019) and the tidyverse package version 2.0.0 (Wickham et al., 2019). We used the patchwork package 1.1.2 (Pedersen, 2020) for creating multiplot arrays, and png version 0.1.8 (Urbanek, 2022) for loading image files. The effsize package 0.8.1 (Torchiano, 2019) was used to compute the standardized effect size measure Cohen's *d*. The package brms 2.19.0 (Bürkner, 2017) is the main workhorse for our inferential statistics, all of which are versions of Bayesian generalized linear models (specifics on statistical models are detailed below). The package tidybayes 3.0.4 (Kay, 2021) was used for additional processing of brms objects. The data and code for all statistical analyses are also available under the following publicly accessible link: https://osf.io/457yb/

4.5 A Comment on Bayesian Analysis

Throughout our data analysis, we use Bayesian inference rather than null hypothesis significance testing (NHST), a particular branch of what is known as "frequentist" statistics. As Bayesian approaches are still not particularly mainstream in cognitive linguistics and beyond, and as they have not been used in observational studies on linguistic synesthesia yet, we want to justify this choice and aid the reader in interpreting the analyses reported below. Our main reason for using a Bayesian framework is that it is widely known to be illogical, in a strict sense, to take a *p*-value as a confirmation of one's hypothesis: this is known as the fallacy of the transposed conditional (see, among many others, Clayton, 2021; Cohen, 1994; Gigerenzer, 2004; Rozeboom, 1960); that is, so-called "hypothesis tests" cannot formally test hypotheses. It has also frequently been pointed out that NHST has never existed in statistics proper, but has been invented by social scientists by merging two frequentist approaches that are in strict logical opposition to each other (e.g., Gigerenzer et al., 1989; Perezgonzalez, 2015). Thus, our primary reason for preferring a Bayesian analysis over NHST is that we are interested in making claims about hypotheses, which requires using an approach that actually affords making inferences from data to hypotheses in a logically consistent manner.

Another reason for preferring Bayesian methods is that they are more easily interpreted, and more likely to be interpreted correctly, than frequentist statistics. For example, it is a common misconception to treat the 95% confidence intervals derived from a frequentist analysis as equivalent with being "95% confident" that a value of interest is included in the interval, what Morey et al. (2016, p. 103) call "the fallacy of placing confidence in confidence intervals." Researchers have a natural tendency to interpret frequentist 95% confidence intervals as if they were Bayesian 95% credible intervals (Hoekstra et al., 2014), even though only the latter actually quantify our uncertainty in a particular value. Thus, we prefer to use the approach that actually follows our natural tendencies of thinking about data and uncertainty. This also means that even readers who are not familiar with Bayesian methods can readily interpret the results we report below, and in fact, even readers completely naïve to Bayesian frameworks are more likely to arrive at a correct interpretation; for example, the 95% Bayesian credible intervals we report throughout our results – in contrast to frequentist confidence intervals – can be interpreted as indicating a certainty of 95%.

Bayesian approaches, in contrast to frequentist approaches, are characterized by having an explicit framework for incorporating prior information ("priors"). Researchers unfamiliar with modern applied Bayesian statistics are often concerned about priors allowing the analyst to tweak results in favor of one's hypothesis. In fact, the opposite is generally true; it is common in modern Bayesian data analysis to specify what are called "weakly informative" or "regularizing" priors that bias results slightly more toward lower values; that is, these priors assume that small effects are more common. In contrast, a corresponding frequentist/NHST analysis assumes that all values are equally probable, which often ends up being less conservative and more prone to overfitting than a corresponding Bayesian analysis because average results are easily swayed by extreme values, even if they stem from small samples. Weakly informative priors allow incorporating a healthy dose of what McElreath (2020, p. 214) calls "mild skepticism" into our analysis. These priors are specified in such a way that if the data strongly suggests a certain pattern, they will impact our conclusions very little, but if there are either weak effects or little data to suggest a strong effect, weakly informative priors bias results more strongly toward zero and thus yield more conservative conclusions than a corresponding frequentist analysis.

Precise prior specifications are detailed within the respective subsections dedicated to each analysis and can also be found in the online repository of our analysis (https://osf.io/457yb/). Importantly, the conclusions we report are not substantially affected by a range of different prior choices.

4.6 Overview of Analyses

Our analyses proceed in four stages, as represented in Table 4. Our overall trajectory is that we start with the grossest measures, those that rely heavily on averages. From there, we progress toward more bottom-up approaches. Thus, our analyses can be conceived as a funnel, starting with the "big picture" and progressively zooming in to more specific patterns. Taken together, our analyses also achieve something else that we believe is important for the study of linguistic synesthesia, which is that we separate analytical questions that are sometimes conflated (as discussed in Section 3.5). Table 4 provides an overview of which research questions each analysis answers.

First, we compute a measure of "hierarchy congruency" from each table of linguistic synesthesias. This answers the question: How many tokens overall, across all cells off the diagonal in each table, are consistent with the proposed hierarchy of the senses? This analysis thus casts a wide net, looking at every intersense transfer that fits the hierarchy, and comparing that to the total number

Table 4 Overview of analyses conducted in our study

Analysis	Shorthand label	Research question
#1	Hierarchy congruency	What percentage of tokens are congruent with the hierarchy?
#2	Source/target ratios	For each modality, does it show a preference to be a source or target?
#3	Pairwise asymmetry	For each modality pair, is the relationship symmetrical or asymmetrical?
#4	Specific mappings	What specific mappings are over-represented?

of attested linguistic synesthesias. In this approach, the contribution of individual cells is ignored by virtue of relying on summary statistics.

Before proceeding to the other analyses, it is worth thinking in more detail how even if an analysis showed a very high percentage of hierarchy-congruent cases, say 80% of all linguistic synesthesias, the actual data patterns that make up this percentage could be inconsistent with our understanding of the hierarchy of senses as a monolithic construct. There are two scenarios, both relevant to our meta-analysis. If *a small number of the same cells across studies* are driving up the average across different studies, this poses problems for the hierarchy of the senses. Under this scenario, the proportion of hierarchy-congruent cases could overly depend on a specific sense pair. A candidate mapping for this that has previously been discussed in the literature is touch→sound, which Ullmann's generalizations already suggest will be statistically dominant. In fact, the propensity of referring to auditory impressions via touch vocabulary has also been noted in other fields, such as in music psychology studies on timbre (see, e.g., Saitis & Weinzierl, 2019; Wallmark, 2019; Wallmark & Kendall, 2018). Similarly, Fónagy (1963) presents a book-length treatment of how touch and sight vocabulary commonly feature in phonetics texts. If touch→sound, or any other specific mapping for that matter, were driving the overall average of hierarchy-congruent cases across studies, explanatory approaches would have to shift from being focused on a monolithic "hierarchy" toward accounting for what explains the over-representation of specific mappings.

The second scenario we have to consider is that *different cells* carry the average proportion in different studies; for example, a high percentage of hierarchy-congruent cases may be based on touch→sound in one study, and on taste→sound in another study, etc. This scenario is equally problematic for the notion of a monolithic hierarchy, as it would suggest that there are in fact author- or language-specific preferences that are averaged over, and only when we cast a net that is as wide as lumping several of the cells in Table 1 together in a single summary statistic does it look as if the hierarchy received support. These two scenarios thus highlight that it is of key theoretical interest to consider the impact of specific mappings. Doing so directly speaks to whether a monolithic hierarchy is actually needed to explain asymmetries observed in linguistic synesthesias. In linguistics and beyond, there is a general move toward paying more attention to the distributional nature of data, and relying less on gross summary statistics (Hehman & Xie, 2021; Speelman & McGann, 2013; Weissgerber et al., 2015). Crucially, the analyses we present below do both: computing averages in analysis #1, as well as looking at more detailed patterns in analyses #2–4 that rely progressively less on coarse averages.

Analysis #2 looks at each sensory modality's propensity to be either a source or a target. This is a modality-focused analysis: for each modality, we compute the ratio of how much it is used as a source over how much it is used as a target, thereby providing a gross measure of source/target asymmetry. Analysis #3 also computes source/target ratios, but not as an average for an entire modality, but separately for each modality *pair*. That is, in this analysis we ask for each combination of two senses: Is the relationship between the two modalities asymmetrical, and if so, by how much? Notice that this analysis is purely focused on relative asymmetry, but disregarding all concerns of absolute frequency (see discussion in Section 3.5). Thus, a particular combination of two senses may appear to be very asymmetrical if it consistently has the same high source/target ratio across studies, but how much this asymmetry contributes to the total of all linguistic synesthesias is a separate question, which analysis #4 will answer. This final analysis is arguably the most bottom-up, in that we directly translate the individual percentages of each cell into a picture of which mappings are most common, without any preconceived notion about the existence of a hierarchy of the senses.

It is worth highlighting again that the questions in Table 4 are often not neatly separated in discussions of linguistic synesthesia (see also Section 3.5). Each question is focused on a different data pattern, which also means that we can reach different conclusions with respect to the hierarchy from each analysis. For example, it is possible that touch is used overall more commonly as a source as opposed to target domain (analysis #2), but despite this, it could have a symmetrical relation with a specific other sense (analysis #3). Or, a pair of two particular senses may exhibit strong asymmetry (analysis #3), but may be rare overall in terms of absolute frequency (analysis #4).

Section 4 discussed the overall methodology and rationale of our meta-analysis. In the following sections, each analysis will be discussed with the corresponding results in return.

5 Analysis #1: Hierarchy Congruency

5.1 Overview

In this section, we focus on the analysis of hierarchy congruency: What percentage of tokens is congruent with the hierarchy?

When computing the number of hierarchy-congruent cases, it is crucial to consider which specific version of the hierarchy is supposed to be taken as the baseline. For example, in the proposal by Williams (1976), smell is not a source modality, only a target (see also Galac & Zayniev, 2023, p. 454); and color and sound are symmetrically connected in his model. Proposals also differ with respect to their assumptions about sight and sound, and whether these perhaps share a position on the hierarchy. Here we will use as a starting point what Winter (2019a) called the "simplified consensus hierarchy," taken to reflect a compromise between varying proposals:

(v) touch > taste > smell > sight/sound

This hierarchy treats sight and sound as equals, which means that both the sight→sound and sound→sight cells in Table 1 are judged to be hierarchy-congruent, in line with the fact that Williams (1976) puts 'color' and 'sound' on the same level of his network representation. Such a consensus hierarchy is a sensible starting point as it has the biggest chance of capturing evidence for a linear hierarchy of the senses, as shown by Winter's (2019a) analysis that tests various versions of the hierarchy with American English data (see also Kumcu, 2021, for Turkish).

We modelled the count of hierarchy-congruent cases out of the total number of tokens using a mixed Bayesian logistic regression in which each data point represents a dataset ($N = 38$). The main model is an intercept-only model, which estimates a single fixed effects term, the overall average proportion of congruent cases. This model also includes random intercepts for language (14 levels). As mentioned in Section 2, the standard way of dealing with genealogical or areal dependencies in linguistic typology is via the inclusion of random effects for language family and language area (e.g., Bentz & Winter, 2014; Cysouw, 2010; Jaeger et al., 2011; Sóskuthy & Roettger, 2020; Winter et al., 2022). This, however, is impossible in the specific case of our meta-analysis because except for Indo-European, we do not have multiple languages per language family, which means that for all these families, the effect of language and the effect of family are inseparable in the data. We therefore have to make do with a simple random effect of language to at least account for the fact that there are multiple dependent data points for each language.

The theoretically most important prior in this specific logistic regression model is that of the intercept: the prior of the intercept encapsulates what values we expect the average % hierarchy-congruency measure to assume before seeing the data. We chose a weakly informative *Normal*(0.2006707, 0.5) prior (a normal distribution with a mean of 0.2006707 and a standard deviation of 0.5), which can be justified as follows: for a 5 × 5 table, there are 25 cells, 5 of which lie on the diagonal and are not relevant for linguistic synesthesia because they represent within-modality mappings (touch→touch, taste→taste etc.). Out of the remaining 20 cells, 11 are congruent with the simplified consensus hierarchy, which includes the 10 cells above the diagonal plus the additional sight→sound cell. If we were to spread out tokens across all cells uniformly, that is, each cell contains the same number of cases, we would therefore expect the percentage of hierarchy-congruent cases to be 11/20 = 55%, which thus serves as a suitable baseline. Logistic regression uses the logit link function, which means that we used a prior that was actually centered on 0.2006707, the logit value corresponding to 55%. The 0.5 standard deviation reflects our prior assumption that variation around this baseline value is to be expected, but values closer to the 55% baseline have higher prior probability. Thus, this weakly informative prior draws intercepts toward chance expectation *unless* there is sufficient data to suggest otherwise.

For the random effects standard deviation (by-language variation), we used a *t*-distributed prior with scale 3, mean 0, and sigma 2.5. Sensitivity analyses suggest that the results presented in Section 5.2 do not depend on prior choices, for example, a uniform prior on the intercept, which is totally agnostic with respect to the average proportion of congruent cases leads to theoretically equivalent conclusions. The results reported can also be obtained on the relatively agnostic default priors of the 'brms' package for this model type.

5.2 Results

5.2.1 Descriptive Statistics

Across all datasets, the average percentage of hierarchy-congruent cases was 91.6%. This mean is a simple average, thus treating all datasets as equal regardless of how many tokens were analyzed. As discussed in Section 4.1, tables vary greatly in the number of tokens. We therefore also computed a mean inversely weighted by the size of the dataset, so that larger datasets can contribute more to the average proportion than smaller samples. This weighted mean was 90.8%, which is only minimally different from the unweighted mean. The percentage of hierarchy-congruent cases was very similar across studies, with the highest being 98.9% by Day (1996), and the lowest being 81.2% by Fujimoto (2001). It is worth pointing out that sample size was weakly correlated with the hierarchy congruency statistic (Spearman's rho = 0.36), which means that larger studies found slightly more support for the hierarchy, compared to smaller studies.

For the corpus datasets, the average percentage of hierarchy-congruent cases was largely the same between those studies investigating general language ($M = 92.5\%$) and those investigating literary language ($M = 91.8\%$). The effect size of the difference between these two genres was indicated to be negligible (Cohen's $d = 0.16$, 95% CI: [−0.74, +1.06]). Similarly, results were almost exactly the same for corpus studies ($M = 91.9\%$) and dictionary studies ($M = 90.5\%$), with the difference between the two being of a "small" effect size ($d = 0.31$, 95% CI: [−0.44, +1.06]). Figure 3 visualizes the proportions separately for genre and type.

To formally assess the impact of the genre and type predictors, we compared models with and without the relative fixed effects in question (either "genre" or "data type") that also controlled for cross-linguistic variation using a random effect for language. For this, we used LOO-CV (leave-one-out cross-validation), a model evaluation metric capturing how well a model can account for unseen data points (Vehtari et al., 2017).[4] For the corpus data which distinguishes genre (28 published datasets), this analysis suggested that the model actually performs better *without* the genre predictor (by 163 expected log pointwise predictive density, ELPD), but the difference between the models is associated with a comparatively large standard error ($SE = 186.7$). Using two times the standard error as a heuristic threshold, the models were not indicated to be significantly different in their ability to predict unseen data. For data type (corpus versus dictionary), the model *with* the type predictor performed better (ELPD difference = 106.6), but this difference was also associated with a large standard error ($SE = 98.9$), indicating that the models do not differ significantly in how well they can capture unseen data. In other words, not much is to be gained from adding the type predictor, just as was the case with genre. The fact that neither "genre" nor "data type" added significant predictive power,

---

[4] For a dataset with N data points, the model is refit N times, each time leaving out one of the data points and assessing to what extent the model fit on the remaining data points can account for the left-out data point.

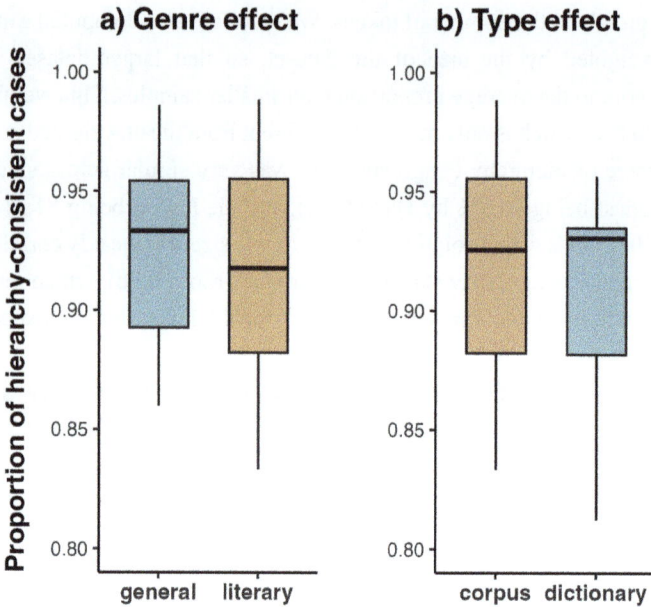

Figure 3 Box plots showing the distribution of the hierarchy congruency statistic across studies (each data point is one study); there are no strong differences between general and literary language (a), and between corpus and dictionary datasets (b); note that the genre effect only characterizes the corpus data as we do not distinguish between genres for the dictionary dataset

alongside the small effect size reported above, licenses our focus on models without these predictors in the following analyses.

5.2.2 Statistical Model of Hierarchy Congruency

The main model without genre and type predictors estimated the average percentage of hierarchy congruency to be 92.2% (posterior mean), with a 95% credible interval ranging from 89.2% to 94.3%. Thus, given this data, model, and priors, we can be 95% certain that the average percentage of hierarchy congruency would lie between these values in any other sample of languages with similar characteristics. When performing a hypothesis test against the chance level (55%), every single posterior estimate of the average proportion was above chance, $p(\beta_0 > 55\%) = 1.0$, indicating that given this model, dataset, and priors, we can be very confident that the meta-analytic average was far removed from our baseline expectation. Figure 4 shows the posterior means for individual languages (black squares) taken from the corresponding Bayesian logistic regression model, with superimposed descriptive

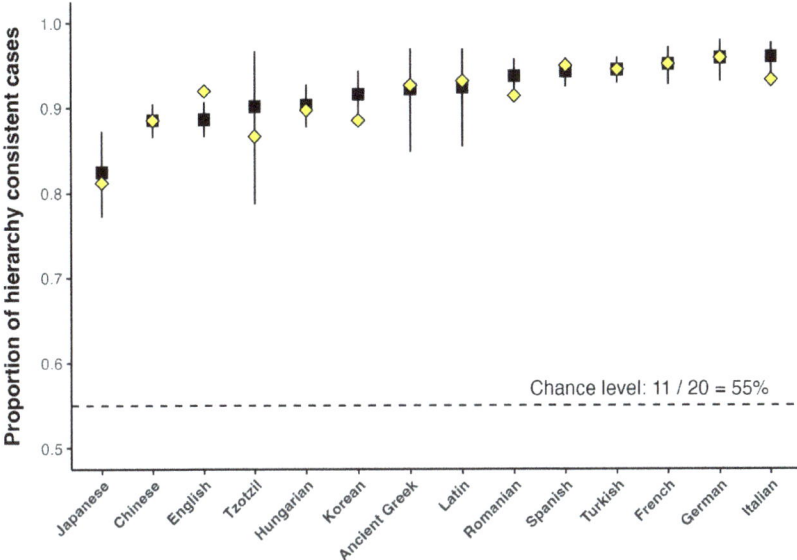

Figure 4 Hierarchy congruency across languages; squares represent posterior means taken from the random effects structure of the main model without type and genre predictors, with whiskers representing 95% credible intervals; yellow diamonds represent descriptive sample means

means (diamond shapes). As can be seen, 95% credible intervals were much wider for languages with smaller datasets, such as Tzotzil. Importantly, not a single interval came even close to overlapping with our chance expectation of 55%, thus reinforcing the idea that this set of languages behaves in a remarkably uniform manner with respect to the hierarchy congruency statistic.

5.2.3 Drivers of Hierarchy Congruency

For each upward transfer that is consistent with the hierarchy, for which we also include sound→sight, we computed the proportion it makes up of the total number of hierarchy-congruent cases separately for each dataset. For instance, in Ullmann's Table 1 above, there are 176 hierarchy-congruent cases as per the simplified consensus hierarchy (i.e., all cells in the upper-right triangle plus sound→sight); of these, 76 cases are from the touch→sound cell, which means that this cell contributes 38.8% (= 76 / 176) to hierarchy congruency for this dataset.

Figure 5 shows the results, ordered from lowest to highest with respect to how much each mapping contributed to hierarchy congruency within each dataset. Each data point in Figure 5 represents a study. As can be seen, touch→sound,

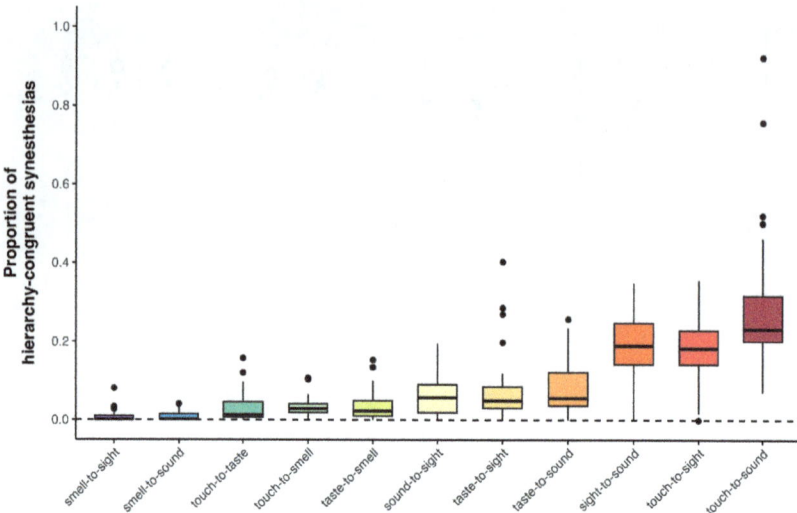

Figure 5 Proportion each upwards transfer (and sound→sight) makes up of the hierarchy-congruent cases, ordered by increasing impact on the average

touch→sight, and sight→sound made up the majority of the hierarchy-congruent cases. Across all datasets, these three specific mappings together made up on average about two-thirds of the hierarchy-congruent cases (65.4%). For some individual datasets, almost the entirety of all hierarchy-congruent cases were just these three mappings: 92.3% for Catricalà's (2008) dictionary analysis of Tzotzil, 84.4% for Day's (1996) analysis of German *Buddenbrooks*, 79.1% of Ullmann's (1947) analysis of literary texts from Théophile Gautier, and 78.7% of Ullmann's (1945) analysis of literary texts from Lord Byron (the same analysis shown in Table 1).

There are other noteworthy patterns visible in Figure 5. It shows that mappings between the lower senses contributed overall very little to hierarchy-congruency, including mappings often presumed to be hierarchy-congruent upward transfers, such as touch→taste, touch→smell, and taste→smell. On the other hand, a mapping between two higher senses, sound→sight, sometimes presumed to be a hierarchy-incongruent downwards transfer, had a much higher proportion than these other mappings. Finally, smell clearly did not contribute much at all to hierarchy congruency across studies. The low proportions for mappings involving smell and taste clearly stem from the low overall counts for these two senses in general language use (see, e.g., Winter et al., 2018). A separate question to which we return below is whether within the relatively few cases that exist for these modalities, mappings exhibit asymmetry (Section 7). Either way, Figure 5 clearly demonstrates the potential of the hierarchy congruency measure to mask the fact that only a handful of cells may be driving the average.

5.2.4 Unidirectionality versus Asymmetry

As mentioned in Section 3.4, we believe that the unidirectionality of a specific mapping (A→B, but never B→A), above and beyond asymmetry (A→B more frequent than B→A), cannot be claimed on the basis of relatively small, finite samples. To assess how data size would change one's conclusions about unidirectionality vis-à-vis asymmetry, we only need to look at the zeros in each table: if for the pair of two modalities A and B, the reverse mapping B→A is never attested, following Zhao et al.'s (2019) reasoning, we would claim that a mapping is unidirectional. However, as is obviously to be expected, the number of cells with zeros that would form the basis of unidirectionality claims correlated inversely with sample size ($rho = -0.62$): studies with more tokens also had less cells with zeros.

Another way to demonstrate the sample size dependent nature of unidirectionality claims is to look at the two languages for which we have the biggest number of tables, English and Hungarian (a total of 8 and 7 tables, respectively). On average, the English tables (from different authors and different studies) had 5.25 zeros. But when aggregating tokens across authors and studies by summing, not a single zero was left. The same was the case for Hungarian: collating all Hungarian tables from Whitney (1952), not a single zero was left, down from on average 4.29 zeros per table prior to summing. This simple analytical exercise shows that not a single reverse mapping is unattested for these two languages once data is aggregated across tables. Moreover, across the entire cross-linguistic sample, not a single cell was ever zero when data was collated. Taken together, these analyses show that linguistic synesthesia is about asymmetry, not unidirectionality.

6 Analysis #2: Source/Target Ratios

6.1 Overview

Analysis #2 answers the question: For each modality, does it show a preference to be a source or target? We do this using source/target ratios. The average source/target ratio for a modality is a simple measure where the row total – how many times a modality is used as source – is divided by the column total – how many times the same modality is used as target (Winter, 2019a, pp. 218–219). Ratios above 1 indicate that a sensory modality lends its vocabulary to the description of sensory impressions from other modalities: the modality is predominantly a source, not a target. Ratios below 1 indicate that the modality is more likely a target. To get a sense for these figures, consider Ullmann's Table 1 shown above, where the stated row and column totals can be used to compute the source/target ratios, which are 15.1 for touch, 2.2 for heat/temperature, 3.4 for taste, 1.0 for smell, 0.09 for sound, and 0.5 for sight. The source/target ratio measure directly addresses Ullmann's generalizations (ii) and (iii); that is, the statement that touch is the most dominant source, and sound is the most dominant target.

In this section, we report logged source/target ratios, which provide an intuitive measure where positive values indicate source preference and negative values indicate target preference. The logged source/target ratios corresponding to Table 1 above are +2.7 for touch, +0.8 for heat/temperature, +1.2 for taste, 0.0 for smell, −2.3 for sound, and −0.7 for sight. Posterior predictive simulations (see online scripts: https://osf.io/457yb/) show that standard Bayesian linear models with a normally distributed data-generating process capture the distribution of these logged ratios well.

Our model of this data included the single fixed effect modality (five levels) and random intercepts for language, as well as modality random slopes for language. No random slopes were needed in analysis #1, which only featured an intercept in the fixed effects. Once we model differences between modalities, however, we need to account for the fact that some modalities may have higher or lower source/target ratios in different languages. The random slopes component of the model captures this by-language variation. This means that, just as is the case with analysis #1, our conclusions stemming from this analysis can be taken to generalize over the set of languages analyzed (cf. Winter & Grice, 2021), although as with analysis #1, it is impossible with this limited sample to formally factor out language family and area variation.

For the model of source/target ratios, we chose a weakly informative *Normal*(0,1) prior for the intercept and all slope coefficients. Just as in analysis #1, this prior is centered on zero and thus has a conservative effect on the data, making the model more skeptical of large effects in the presence of weak evidence. We used a *t*-distributed prior (scale 3, center 0, and 2.5 sigma) for all standard deviation terms, and an *LKJ*(2) prior for the random effects correlations (in this case, a single intercept/slope correlation term). Just as with analysis #1, our substantive conclusions do not change fundamentally if different prior assumptions are implemented, such as agnostic uniform priors on slope terms.

6.2 Results

6.2.1 Descriptive Statistics

We computed the source/target ratios separately for each sensory modality and separately for each dataset. Across all datasets, the average source/target ratio for each modality was 20.3 for touch, 11.0 for taste, 0.40 for smell, 0.18 for sound, and 0.98 for sight. The corresponding log ratios were: +2.37 for touch, +1.75 for taste, −1.32 for smell, −2.20 for sound, and −0.39 for sight. These values indicate that touch and taste were on average more likely to be sources,

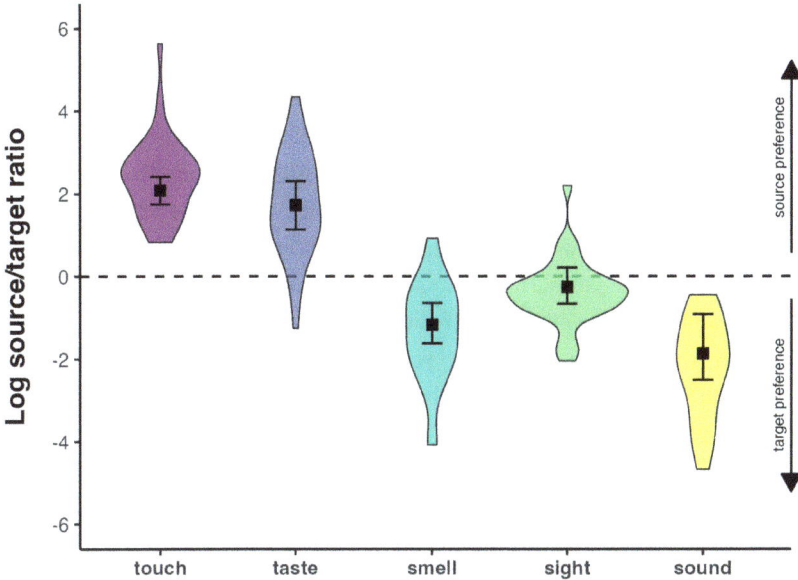

Figure 6 Log source/target ratios for the five senses (each data point is one dataset); values above 0 mean that a given modality is more likely a source than a target; values below 0 mean that a given modality is more likely a target than a source; error bars plot 95% credible intervals taken from the model described in Section 6.1; since this model incorporates a language random effect, these intervals also incorporate cross-linguistic variation

and smell and sound were on average more likely to be targets. Sight shows a very mild target preference, but was overall more symmetrical in its profile.

Figure 6 shows the distribution of all log ratios for each of the five senses, with each data point representing one dataset. The dashed midline corresponds to symmetry, that is, a source/target ratio of 1.0 (and hence a logarithm of 0). Given that the majority of datasets in this sample come from different languages, this means that the overall spread of all data points in this figure can also be taken as a rough visual proxy for linguistic variation. The figure shows that only touch was more likely to be a source than target in all datasets without exception. For taste, three datasets (English, Latin, and Ancient Greek) from Catricalà (2008) exhibited negative log source/target ratios. In stark contrast to taste, smell featured as a dominant source in only two datasets (Heany in Bretones-Callejas, 2001; Keats in Ullmann, 1945), and it otherwise showed a preference for being a target. Sight showed source preference in some datasets, but was overall more prone to being a target. Finally, sound was a dominant target in *all* datasets, without exception: in not a single dataset was sound more commonly used as source.

6.2.2 Statistical Model of Source/Target Ratios

The 95% credible intervals in Figure 6 give an indication of how much uncertainty we have in a modality's relative source or target preference, given the Bayesian linear mixed effects model with random effect for language (see Section 6.1), which means that just as was the case for analysis #1, this analysis also formally generalizes over languages. As can be seen from the overlap, the 95% credible interval for sight firmly included zero, which means that given this model, data, and priors, sight on average showed no preference for being either a source or a target in linguistic synesthesia. The other 95% credible intervals clearly excluded zero. We performed hypothesis tests against zero separately for each modality to quantify each modality's posterior probability of being either source- or target-biased. The posterior probability of touch and taste having source preference was exactly 1, $p(touch|taste) > 0 = 1.0$, which means that based on this model, prior and data, we can be very confident that these two modalities show source preference. For smell and sound, the pattern was reversed: both were associated with a very high certainty of being more commonly a target, $p(smell|sound < 0) = 1.0$. As the overlapping credible interval already suggested, only for sight did this hypothesis test obtain less certain results; its posterior probability of being a more likely target is $p(sight < 0) = 0.88$. We can thus say that given this model, data, and priors, there was a 12% chance that the mean may lie on the other side of the midline (Figure 6, dashed). While this shows a clear numerical trend for sight to be target-biased, these results indicate that compared to the other senses, we are considerably more uncertain about any preferences of sight.

In yielding a singular value associated with each modality, the source/target ratio analysis presented here allows lining up the senses in linear order, from relative source to relative target preference. This allows comparing a model with the five-level predictor "modality" to an otherwise equivalent model with a simplified fixed effect for "hierarchy" that has two levels, separating the lower senses (touch, taste, smell) from the higher ones (sight, sound). LOO-CV comparison between these models (see Section 5.2.1) indicates that the model with the hierarchy predictor performed significantly worse than the model that captures each modality separately (ELPD difference = −79.5, standard error of difference = 9.1). The models also differed starkly in R^2 (described variance): the "hierarchy" model described only 28.7% of the variance in source/target ratios. In contrast, the "modality" model described 73.5% of the variance. All of this makes sense given the patterns that we have seen in Figure 6: smell in particular, being a much more likely target than source, did not neatly pattern together with the other presumed-to-be "lower" senses of touch and taste. In fact, in its propensity to be a target, smell was most similar to the "higher" modality of sound. This shows that the binary divide of separating the sensorium into "lower" and "higher" senses does not work well for characterizing which senses are more likely sources, and which are more likely targets.

6.2.3 Diversity of Targets

Alongside our analysis of source/target ratios, we also computed a single-valued diversity statistic that allows us to capture whether a given source modality mapped strongly onto only one or a couple of targets, or whether it showed a relatively more diverse range of targets. Diversity can be computed using Shannon entropy, $H = -\sum p(x)\log p(x)$, which is maximal for a uniform distribution of targets (e.g., for the set {25, 25, 25, 25}: $H = 1.39$) and assumes lower values the more strongly just one target is preferred (e.g., for the set {80, 5, 5, 5}: $H = 0.61$). We analyzed these entropies with a Bayesian linear model of the same structure as our source/target ratio analysis (the priors were kept the same as variables have similar scales), including the same language random effect to allow for cross-linguistic generalization.

The results are shown in Figure 7. In the average, these entropies were 1.24 for smell, 1.19 for taste, followed by 1.01 for touch, 1.01 for sight, and 0.78 for sound. It is worth focusing here on the contrast between touch and taste, both of which the

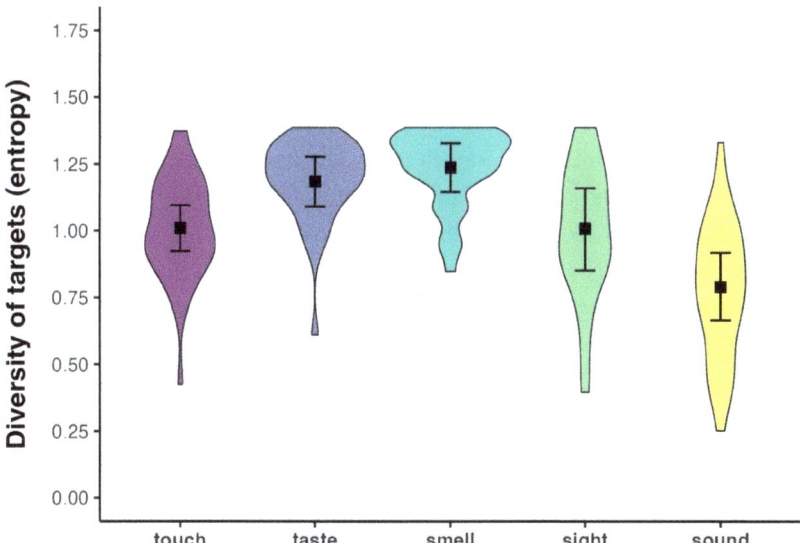

Figure 7 Diversity of targets as measured by Shannon entropy over target cells per row; squares represent posterior means from the corresponding Bayesian model; error bars indicate 95% credible intervals and incorporate cross-linguistic variation due to the model for this data featuring language random effects

source/target ratio analysis indicated to have source preference. The fact that taste had higher entropy than touch means that it attached to a wider range of targets, or conversely, that touch demonstrated a stronger preference for more specific targets (specifically, touch→sound and touch→sight, as shown in analysis #1). The high entropy of smell suggests that its pattern of targets was diffuse, if in fact it was ever used as source, which as the above results showed did not happen very often anyway. Notice that sound showed the lowest target entropy. This stems from the fact that when it featured as a source in linguistic synesthesia at all, the target was almost always sight; that is, sound→sight dominated all mappings in which sound featured as a source.

7 Analysis #3: Pairwise Asymmetry

7.1 Overview

This analysis answers the question: For each modality pair, is the relationship symmetrical or asymmetrical? This analysis follows a similar logic to the source/target ratios, except that the ratios are not computed on the basis of row and column totals, but pairwise for each combination of two senses. In Table 1 above, touch was used to talk about sight 31 times, and sight was used to talk about touch 5 times, thus yielding a pairwise source/target ratio of 6.2. This computation, however, introduces a problem when tables feature cells that contain zeros, such as was the case with Table 1 above. Since ratios cannot be computed when the denominator is zero, we uniformly added +1 to all cells for this analysis only. So, for the touch/sound pair in Table 1, the touch→sound cell would have 77 tokens; the sound→touch cell would have 1 token. This made it possible to compute the source/target ratio for this pair as 77/1 = 77.0. As we have done for analysis #3, we logarithmically transformed these ratios, which means that positive values indicate that A→B is more frequent than B→A, and negative values indicate the reverse. We entered these asymmetry scores into a Bayesian linear model with a fixed effect for pair (10 levels, one for each sensory modality pair), as well as random intercepts and by-pair random slopes for language. By featuring a random effect for language, this analysis generalizes across languages just as was the case with analysis #1 and #2. As the pairwise asymmetry ratios were scaled similarly to analysis #2, we reused the same priors.

7.2 Results

Figure 8 shows the resultant log/source target ratios and their 95% credible intervals taken from the Bayesian model generalizing over languages. Whichever modality

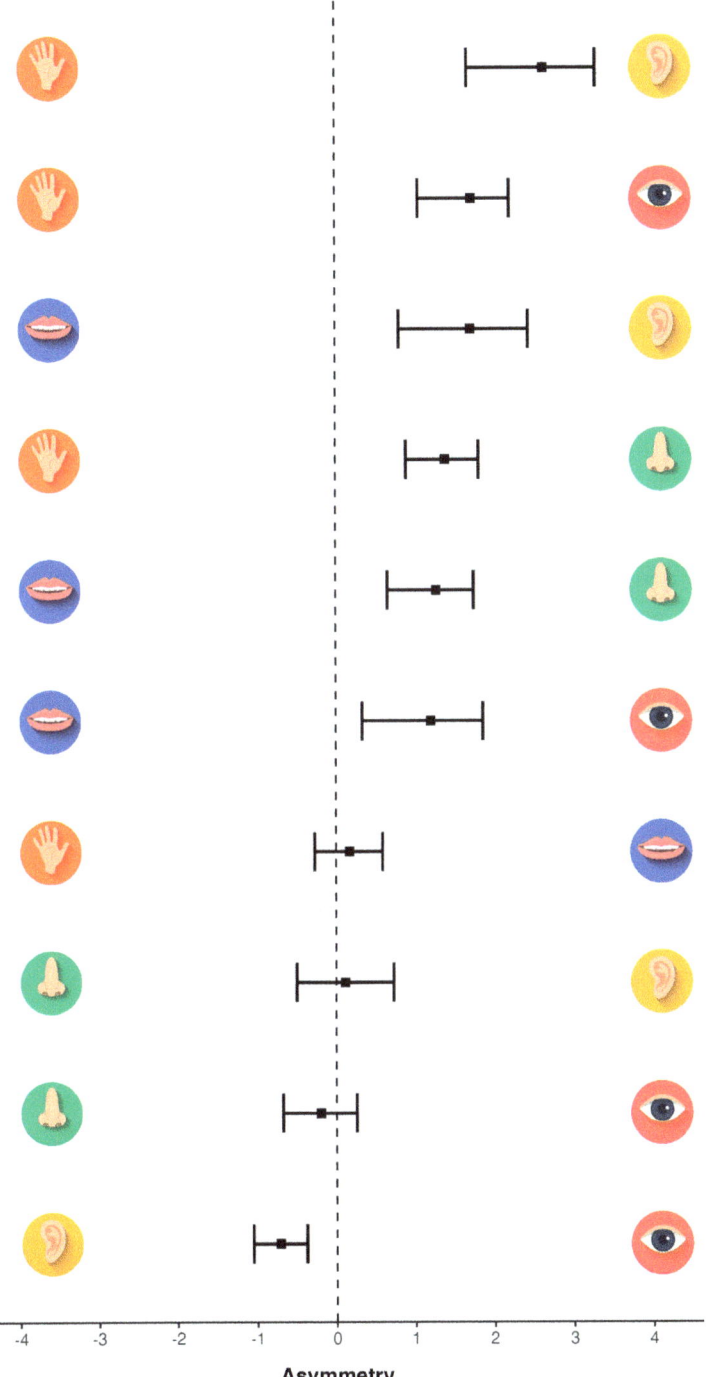

Figure 8 Log source/target asymmetries separately for each pair of sensory modalities; squares (posterior means) and error bars (95% credible intervals) are taken from the corresponding Bayesian linear mixed effects model, described in Section 7.1; thanks to including a random effect, these error bars also incorporate cross-linguistic variation

the posterior mean (black square) is closer to was the more likely target for each pair in this analysis.

Figure 8 shows that touch and sound exhibited the most pronounced pairwise asymmetry, followed by touch→sight, taste→sound, touch→smell, taste→smell, taste→sight, and finally sight→sound. For each of these mappings, the 95% interval clearly excluded zero (= symmetry), which means that we can be very certain that this analysis has correctly captured the directionality of the asymmetry; that is, we are very certain that touch→sound is more common than sound→touch, and so on. It is important to keep in mind, however, that these ratios cancel out absolute frequencies (Section 3.5). For example, even though taste→smell was indicated to be highly asymmetrical, as shown in Figure 8, whether this mapping was also frequent is a separate question, which is the focus of the next analysis, analysis #4.

8 Analysis #4: Specific Mappings

8.1 Overview

The final analysis answers the question: What specific mappings are over-represented? This analysis arguably provides the least filtered and most bottom-up perspective of the available data: we simply computed the proportion of each cell, taken out of the total number of linguistic synesthesias for each table. By not performing any ratio calculations as in analyses #2 and #3, this analysis also directly addresses absolute frequency, as discussed in Section 3.5.

8.2 Results

8.2.1 Descriptive Statistics

Table 5 shows the percentage of all data points in each cell averaged across all studies in our meta-analysis. After aggregating the data, smell was indicated to barely ever be a source at all, with source percentages for this modality being effectively zero. Table 5 also shows a picture that was already preempted by our analysis of which cells contributed most to the hierarchy congruency measure (Section 5.2.3): touch→sound, touch→sight, and sight→sound greatly dominate the picture, relative to the other mappings. Following this, we see slightly fewer instances of taste→sight and taste→sound.

The precise proportion of each mapping was, of course, different for each study. This variation across studies is not reflected in Table 5 since these percentages average out all variation across datasets, and across languages. Ignoring this variation naturally leads to overconfident conclusions as variation

Table 5 Percentages of linguistic synesthesias, averaged across all datasets; row and column margins indicate summed percentage points; percentages do not add up to 100% due to rounding

	Touch	Taste	Smell	Sound	Sight	Total
Touch	(-)	1%	3%	22%	18%	44%
Taste	2%	(-)	4%	7%	11%	24%
Smell	-	-	(-)	-	-	0%
Sound	-	-	-	(-)	2%	2%
Sight	5%	1%	1%	21%	(-)	28%
	7%	2%	8%	50%	31%	100%

translates into uncertainty when doing inferential statistics. For example, even if a particular cell has a high average percentage, we may be uncertain about this percentage being high if there are also many studies which show low values. To tackle this, the following section describes a statistical model of the percentages shown in Figure 5.

8.2.2 Statistical Model

To add uncertainty information to Table 5, we used a mixed beta regression model of proportions. The beta distribution is continuous and bounded by [0, 1], which makes it a suitable data-generating process for modeling proportions. This beta regression model included the fixed effect 'mapping' with 20 levels, one for each specific cell seen in Table 5 (touch→taste, touch→smell, ..., taste→touch etc.). We allowed the phi parameter of the beta distribution, which models variance in beta regression, to also differ between these levels; that is, we modeled both the average proportion of each cell as well as the variation in proportions as dependent on each mapping. As before, the model contained a random effect for language, including both random intercept and random slope variation (by-language variation in the effect of 'mapping'). This means that just as with the previous analyses, the results reported below formally generalize over cross-linguistic variation.

Table 6 shows the resulting proportions taken from the model (converted to percentages). In contrast to Table 5, these percentages and their 95% intervals take study variation and language variation into account. The bracketed values indicate the corresponding 95% credible intervals taken from the model. We use color highlighting to show what cells account for

Table 6 Percentages of each mapping out of the total number of linguistic synesthesias, based on posterior means extracted from mixed beta regression model: dark green highlights percentages >10%, and light green highlights percentages >5%; brackets contain 95% credible intervals taken from the corresponding mixed beta regression model that includes a language random effect and thus incorporates cross-linguistic variation

	Touch	Taste	Smell	Sound	Sight
Touch	(-)	2.8% [1.6%, 5.2%]	2.6% [1.6%, 4.0%]	25.5% [14.8%, 39.4%]	14.3% [9.2%, 20.2%]
Taste	1.5% [0.9%, 2.5%]	(-)	2.9% [1.7%, 4.8%]	6.4% [3.9%, 9.8%]	6.2% [3.7%, 10.1%]
Smell	0.2% [0.1%, 0.5%]	0.2% [0.1%, 0.4%]	(-)	0.8% [0.4%, 1.4%]	0.7% [0.4%, 1.4%]
Sound	1.0% [0.5%, 1.9%]	0.2% [0.1%, 0.4%]	0.5% [0.3%, 0.9%]	(-)	5.5% [3.8%, 8.0%]
Sight	2.3% [1.3%, 4.2%]	1.0% [0.5%, 2.1%]	0.7% [0.4%, 1.4%]	15.5% [10.6%, 22.3%]	(-)

more than 10% of cases (dark green), or more than 5% (light green) in their average (posterior mean).

The overall picture is quite similar to the descriptive averages reported in the last section, but after controlling for language, certain modalities had higher or lower values relative to Table 5; for example, touch→sound cell was relatively higher, and touch→sight relatively lower. It is noteworthy that for some cells, our beta regression indicated uncertainty to be quite high. For example, the 95% credible interval for the touch→sound cell was indicated to be [14.8%, 39.4%]. This means that given this model, data, and priors, a value as low as 14.8% is still compatible with the data, and so is a value as high as 39.4%. The relatively high width of some of these credible intervals is not only due to variation within the cells across studies and languages but also due to the fact that 38 datasets is an overall small sample size, especially when compared to some other typological studies.[5]

Figure 9 is based on the values shown in Table 6, which we translated into a diagrammatic representation that shows the overarching patterns of this

---

[5] Cells with overall higher percentages also show wider 95% credible intervals. This is to be expected given that percentages have a natural lower bound at 0%, which constrains variation for cells that have overall lower numbers across datasets.

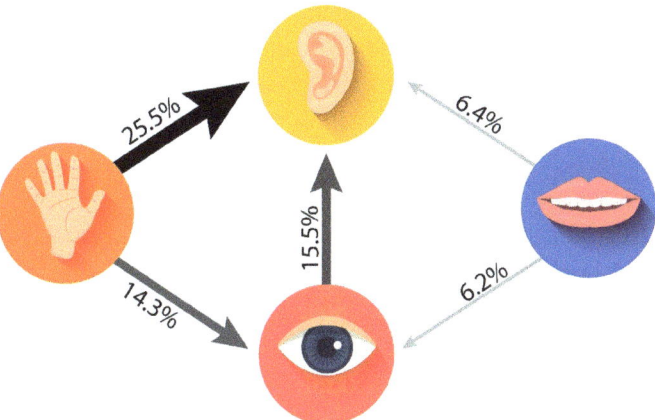

Figure 9 Network of intersensory transfers that exceed 5% of all linguistic synesthesias with at least 80% certainty; both arrow strength and color maps onto the magnitude of the transfer (largest darkest arrow = 25.5%)

analysis. We constructed this figure as follows: for each cell, we computed whether we could be at least 80% certain that the percentage of the cell exceeded 5%. If certainty exceeded the heuristic threshold of 80%, the connection between the senses was indicated by an arrow pointing from source to target. We chose 5% as baseline since each cell would contain this value if percentages were spread uniformly across all cells. The sound→sight cell indicated to be light green in Table 6 is missing from Figure 9 because the posterior probability of this cell being above 5% was only 0.69; that is, we cannot be particularly certain that this cell exceeds the 5% threshold given this data, model, and priors.

9 Discussion

9.1 Summary of Results

Our analyses investigated data from nearly a century's worth of research on linguistic synesthesia from four analytical perspectives. In this section, we summarize this complex picture of results, and take stock of how the theoretical construct of a linear hierarchy of the senses, or a binary divide between lower and higher senses, fares in the context of these analyses. How do the empirical results from analyses #1–4 speak to our understanding of the hierarchy?

With a simple measure of hierarchy congruency, our meta-analysis looked, upon first inspection, as if it strongly supported the notion of the hierarchy of the senses. That is, when all the cells were lumped together into an aggregate measure, there were overall more hierarchy-congruent cases than hierarchy-incongruent cases. It could seem like a remarkable success story for the hierarchy that congruency was overall very high (around 90% on average), and that this pattern was very consistent across the 14 languages featuring in our meta-analysis. In fact, even for the dataset with the lowest percentage, hierarchy congruency was still over 80%.

The hierarchy congruency analysis also showed that neither genre (literary versus general language) nor data type (corpus versus dictionary) mattered much. As discussed in Section 4.1, dictionaries encode word types, whereas corpora include tokens. The fact that both types of data showed similar results suggests that linguistic synesthesia is lexically productive and does not hinge on specific lexical items as much. This is also independently corroborated by studies which explicitly compare types and tokens of linguistic synesthesias (Kumcu, 2021; Ronga et al., 2012; Winter, 2019a). The absence of genre and data type effects also speaks to the idea that linguistic synesthesia patterns similarly for highly creative and less creative language use: it can be assumed that literary texts contain relatively more novel linguistic synesthesias than general language, which itself can be assumed to contain more novel synesthesias than dictionaries. The absence of any differences between these categories thus suggests that novel and conventional synesthesias behave similarly, although a more direct test of this idea is needed to confirm this result more explicitly.

We also demonstrated that the hierarchy congruency analysis has a major flaw: averages can be deceiving. Summing up the entire upper triangle of Table 1 (plus the sight→sound cell in the lower triangle) casts a very wide net, masking the contribution of individual cells to the average. In fact, we found that out of the 11 cells that were treated as hierarchy-congruent, only three mappings – touch→sound, touch→sight, and sight→sound – drive the average, accounting for overall two-thirds of hierarchy congruency. Among these mappings, sight→sound is not even captured by statements claiming that linguistic synesthesia goes from lower to higher senses; that is, this specific mapping would not be treated as a lower-to-higher transfer in some proposals. These results suggest that much of what is generally attributed to the hierarchy can be captured with a much smaller set of mappings.

Our second analytical approach used source/target ratios, which allowed us to separate those sensory modalities that were predominant lenders of vocabulary from those that are predominant borrowers. In this analysis, touch and taste emerged as showing strong preferences for being sources in linguistic synesthesia, and sound and smell emerged as showing strong preferences for being targets; sight had a more symmetrical profile, showing target preference in many studies, but also source preference in others. If we were to rank-order the average source/target ratios to attempt deriving a linear ordering of the senses, it would be touch > taste > sight > smell > sound. Neither the fact that sight is lower than sound in this ranking nor the fact that smell behaves much unlike the other two purportedly lower senses and patterns more like the presumed-to-be higher modality of sound is captured in how the hierarchy is commonly formulated. We find it particularly striking that the presumed-to-be lower sense of smell shows similar target preference to the "higher" sense of sound. The diversity analysis furthermore showed touch to be of relatively low diversity, which together with the other results indicates its preference for specific sensory modalities, in particular sound and sight.

Our third analytical approach looked at each and every combination of two senses, finding a number of pairwise asymmetries that are consistent across studies and languages. This analysis found that the strongest asymmetry characterizes touch→sound. Importantly, this analysis is best juxtaposed with analysis #4, so that we don't lose sight of which asymmetrical pairs are also frequent. For example, taste→smell is quite asymmetric, in that transfers involving these two modalities consistently tend to feature taste as source, and smell as target, but our fourth and final analysis shows that this mapping is overall very infrequent. The pairwise asymmetries in Figure 8 are hence best read as *if*-statements of the following form: *if* taste and smell feature together in linguistic synesthesia, taste will be the source.

On the basis of looking at the frequencies of all individual cells, our fourth and final analysis arrived at the network visualized in Figure 9. At first sight, this picture could be taken to support the hierarchy of the senses. After all, it is the case that the two source modalities in this diagram are touch and taste, both of which are traditionally considered to be lower senses. Similarly, the presumed-to-be higher senses of sound and sight emerge as targets. But most data patterns even in this diagram are not predicted by standard characterizations of the hierarchy. For example, sight→sound is more than twice as frequent as taste→sound and taste→sight. And, as discussed in Section 3.5, common formulations of the hierarchy are also silent about why sound is a more likely target than sight and why specifically sight is such a common source for sound. In addition, as discussed in Sections 3.4–3.5, we need to consider both asymmetry and overall frequency as continuous metrics. Here, too, the hierarchy falls short of making precise predictions, given that it has nothing to say about why certain lower-to-higher transfers are much more frequent than others in our meta-analysis, such as touch→sound, which is on average 4 times as frequent as taste→sound or taste→sight. A simple linear order, or a lower/higher divide, does not capture these large differences in frequency very well.

Our results clearly show that no matter what analysis we use, the hierarchy of the senses is lacking in making precise predictions for the data patterns we see in our meta-analysis. We believe that the following list captures the generalizations that are actually supported by observational studies on linguistic synesthesia:

a) Touch and taste show a clear source preference
b) Sound and smell show a clear target preference
c) The three specific mappings touch→sound, sight→sound, and touch→sight dominate linguistic synesthesia, in this order
d) Smell rarely features in linguistic synesthesia, but *if* it does, it shows strong asymmetry with taste and touch (taste→smell, touch→smell)

We believe that these four generalizations, together with the diagram shown in Figure 9, help us characterize the explanatory target in research on linguistic synesthesia more precisely. When generalizations are listed this way, we can immediately appreciate that any classification of senses into "lower" and "higher" is not needed, and in fact, would contradict some of the generalizations, for example, vis-à-vis smell and sound. Moreover, there is nothing linear about any of these generalizations; that is, the senses clearly do not fall onto a neat cline.

Finally, it should be said that generalizations (a–d) do not include any unidirectional tendencies; that is, we take our results to be about relative asymmetry (e.g., touch is more likely a source, but it sometimes also is a target) rather than to be about strict unidirectionality (e.g., touch is only a source, never a target). As discussed in the introduction, Zhao et al. (2019) present data from a corpus analysis that they take to be positive evidence for the unidirectionality of some mappings in Chinese, but our analysis shows that unidirectionality is too flimsy a notion to be of theoretical worth as it entirely depends on sample size. Following the credo that "absence of evidence is not evidence of absence," we have shown that once we have more data, all exceptionless unidirectionalities are demoted to asymmetries.

9.2 Away from the Hierarchy, toward Networks

One of the most striking patterns we see in our data is the fact that touch, already a dominant source modality anyway, is particularly attached to sound as a target. Interestingly, in typological research on perception verbs, it has also been found that touch and hearing are the most frequently colexified modalities (Norcliffe & Majid, 2024). That is, across languages, verbs denoting auditory perception also often denote tactile perception. Similarly, Fishman (2022) performed an experiment on analogies such as *The picture looks like my music sounds* that combine terms associated with different sensory modalities (*picture* versus *sound*). Very similar to our results, he found that specifically touch→sound and sight→sound received significantly higher naturalness ratings.[6] Largely independent of linguistic research on this topic, the widespread use of touch vocabulary has also been noticed in music psychology, particularly in research on timbre (Saitis & Weinzierl, 2019; Wallmark, 2019; Wallmark & Kendall, 2018). Why does specifically touch→sound come up again and again as a dominant mapping, including *all* 38 datasets presented here, the perception verbs analyzed by Norcliffe and Majid (2024), the analogies investigated by Fishman (2022), and the psychological literature on timbre? We believe that this question is in much more dire need of explaining than any presumed hierarchical tendencies, given that we show how much of what is generally attributed to the hierarchy is driven by this mapping. The case of touch→sound alone clearly highlights the need to shift away from trying to lump multiple senses together under vague descriptors such as "lower" and "higher" senses, toward more network-based representations that highlight which specific mappings are overrepresented.

We want to argue that, given the patterns uncovered by our meta-analysis, it is theoretically fruitful to consider the senses as forming an interconnected network, rather than a hierarchy. This suggestion mirrors how in linguistic typology, Viberg's "hierarchy" of perception verbs has been updated within the conceptual framework of semantic maps (Norcliffe & Majid, 2024).[7] In parallel, quantitative studies of sensory language more generally have characterized interconnections between the senses in terms of semantic maps (Alvarado et al., 2024) or clustered representations (Winter, 2019a), altogether showing a shift away from a monolithic picture of the senses. Representations of asymmetries in linguistic synesthesia have already moved away from linear hierarchies toward more network-based representations (Shinohara & Nakayama, 2011; Strik-Lievers, 2015; Werning et al., 2006) that visualize specific intersense combinations, such as Kumcu's (2021) chord diagram of asymmetries in Turkish linguistic synesthesias. In fact, representations of the asymmetrical tendencies between the senses have already been network-representations for quite a while anyway, such as Williams' (1976) model, reproduced here with examples in Figure 10. While this diagram was meant to capture a different type

---

[6] A caveat with Fishman's (2022) results is that his statistical analysis does not include a random effect for item, which means that results do not formally generalize over item variation and could be driven by particular items (Clark, 1973; Winter & Grice, 2021).

[7] Indeed, in his original study, Viberg (1983) already included a "refinement" (p. 147) of the hierarchy that we would nowadays describe as a semantic map or network.

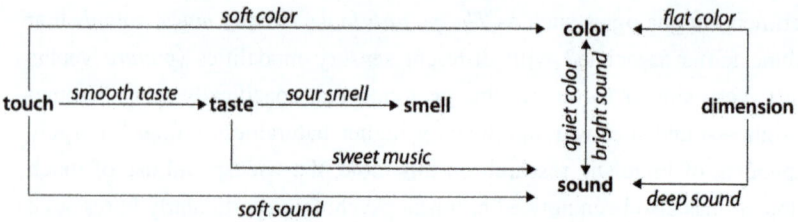

Figure 10 Diagram of transfers from Williams (1976, p. 463), with English examples; figure adapted from Winter (2019a, p. 100)

of generalization – the direction of meaning extension in semantic change as derived from polysemy patterns in dictionary data – it is clear that "network" is a more apt descriptor of this diagram than "hierarchy," a term that together with "hierarchical" never occurs in William's widely cited paper. Yet, despite representations having been more network-based and less hierarchical for quite some time now, researchers use verbal statements that refer to transfers as going from "lower" to "higher" senses (Jo, 2018, p. 38; Shen & Cohen, 1998, p. 123; Zhong et al., 2023, pp. 1–2) to characterize linguistic synesthesia, or that describe asymmetries in linguistic synesthesia as falling on a "linear" cline (Jo, 2022, p. 284; Kumcu, 2021, p. 241; Zhong et al., 2023, p. 3). Our meta-analysis clearly shows that such verbal statements fundamentally do not describe the extant data very well. In addition, our discussion here highlights how such statements are equally at odds with the diagrammatic representations that already had wide currency in this literature.

It is equally important to emphasize that while Ullmann (1937, 1945, 1946, 1947, 1959) ordered his tables with rows and columns in order of touch, temperature/heat, taste, smell, sound and sight, the specifically linear interpretation of the hierarchy seems to originate with Viberg (1983), who essentially took the order of rows/columns in Ullmann's tables and modeled this after the implicational hierarchies that exist in linguistic typology. In fact, our own work has been guilty of falsely attributing the specific diagram used by Viberg (1983) to Ullmann's work (e.g., Strik-Lievers, 2015, p. 71; Winter, 2019a, p. 99), even though Ullmann's analysis and discussion is less strictly linear. It should be emphasized that the generalizations we derive from our meta-analysis described in Section 9.1 are fundamentally more similar to Ullmann's original generalizations than they are to later, more hierarchical reinterpretations of his account.

9.3 Revisiting the Hierarchy as Explanatory Account

As mentioned in the introduction, our analyses provide a new characterization of the explanandum – the phenomenon to be explained – which in turn sets new demands on the explanans – the theory adduced to explain the phenomenon. If there are patterns in the data that the hierarchy does not speak to (such as the dominance of specific mappings like touch→sound and sight→sound), or if there are patterns in the data that the hierarchy makes false predictions for (such as smell patterning like sound in terms of target preference), we can safely conclude that there are no compelling patterns in the data that would strongly call for explanations in terms of the proposed hierarchy. Instead, the generalizations (a–d) resulting from our meta-analysis stated in Section 9.1 shift the focus toward more specific questions that need answering, such as: What explains the dominance of the touch→sound mapping? What explains the affinity of sight and sound in linguistic synesthesia, and more specifically, the dominance of the sight→sound mapping? Why are touch and taste such dominant source domains? Why does smell feature as a target when it occurs in linguistic synesthesia?

In asking these different questions, we automatically shift from a "global" account of asymmetries in linguistic synesthesia to "local" accounts. As discussed in Winter (2019a, p. 105), local accounts seek explanations for specific sensory mappings that are found to be over-represented in the data, or for the influence of specific variables that influence some asymmetries, but not all. On the other hand, global accounts, such as the hierarchy of the senses, seek a "one-size-fits-all" principle that explains the data in a more monolithic manner (for a useful discussion, see also Fishman, 2022). As we have seen in our meta-analysis, the patterns that are actually in the data do not fit monolithic accounts very well; the patterns are clearly too diverse, and too specific to particular senses and sense combinations, that a monolithic explanation would even seem to be a fruitful endeavor.

To understand how explanatory accounts for local as opposed to global accounts differ, it is worth looking at a specific proposal of the more "monolithic" type in more detail. Zhong et al. (2023, pp. 1–2) provide the following explanation, which is one example of a global account that can be found in the literature:

> [...] the directionality of linguistic synesthesia is accounted for in terms of the constraints on mapping from a more concrete concept to a more abstract concept, that is, using a more concrete concept to describe a more abstract concept (Shen 1997; Ullmann [1959]; Williams 1976). Linguistic synesthetic [sic] is thus argued to follow a particular directional pattern, from "lower" or "more embodied" senses (e.g., TOUCH, TASTE, and SMELL) to "higher" or "less embodied" senses (e.g., VISION and HEARING). This account of mapping directionality based on the degree of embodiment is now widely adopted in theories of metaphor such as Conceptual Metaphor Theory (CMT; Lakoff and Johnson 1980, 1999). The degree of the embodiment can be

interpreted as the involvement and/or closeness of bodily contact with the particular sensory organ (Shen 1997; Shen and Aisenman 2008), or to do with subjective (rather than objective) information (Popova 2005), among other interpretations. For instance, lexical items from the tactile (and gustatory) sense that are consistently found to modify items from other senses (e.g., visual and auditory senses) can be explained by substantial involvement of bodily contact as well as references to subjective feelings of the tactile and gustatory senses rather than objective information as perceived by visual and auditory senses.

There are many things of note in this passage. First of all, Ullmann did *not* in fact claim that mappings go from more "concrete" to "abstract"; he did not use these terms and instead spoke of more or less differentiated domains, which is a notion that is wholly different from concreteness. We take these to be the same kind of modern reinterpretation that has happened when Viberg first presented a linear diagram and attributed it to Ullmann, with other researchers since then, including ourselves, following suit with this misinterpretation of past work. It is also worth noting that both Williams and Ullmann actively considered multiple competing explanations, as discussed in Winter (2019a, Ch. 8), and did not commit to any one of them being the dominant factor, yet both authors are cited here and elsewhere in support of modern-day reinterpretations of the generalizations originally made by Ullmann.

Second, while it may sound plausible that body contact or subjectivity could be behind the tendencies observed in linguistic data, we have no way of knowing that this is what actually explains the data, and there are other principles that are equally plausible candidates for motivating the observed asymmetries. The following is a short list of just some of the differences between the senses that could be candidates for motivating the asymmetries between the senses: the senses differ along many dimensions, including:

- which sensory experiences each sense provides access to (e.g., only vision provides access to color, but touch, sight, and to some extent sound provide access to such "common sensibles" as size or roughness; Marks, 1978)
- how precise each sense is for perceiving particular sensory characteristics (e.g., sound is temporally more precise than sight; Ortega et al., 2014)
- how susceptible each sense is to external influences (e.g., smell has been found to be very suggestible by, for example, linguistic context; Case et al., 2006)
- how much information can be captured simultaneously by a sense (e.g., sight allows capturing many things in an instant that would have to be accessed piecemeal with touch)

- how much each sense interacts with emotion (e.g., taste and smell words are more strongly affectively loaded than words associated with the other senses; Winter, 2016)
- whether a sense allows accessing sensory percepts at a distance (e.g., smell, sound, and sight have further reach than touch and taste)
- whether perceptual experiences are easy to intersubjectively verify or not (e.g., English speakers agree more on color labels than smell labels; Majid & Burenhult, 2014)
- how much each sense is valued in different cultures (e.g., Classen, 1993)
- how much communicative need there is to talk about a particular sense (e.g., Winter et al., 2018)
- how codable each sense is in language (e.g., Levinson & Majid, 2014; Majid et al., 2018)
- what other linguistic strategies are available for talking about perceptual experiences associated with a particular sense (e.g., Winter, 2019a, Ch. 3)
- whether a particular sense has an affinity for a particular lexical category (e.g., in some datasets, sound has fewer nouns and more adjectives; Strik-Lievers, 2015; see also Strik-Lievers & Winter, 2018)

And many more. This list is just a small sample of some of the perceptual and linguistic dimensions along which the senses and sensory vocabulary vary. Given the wealth of differences between the senses, as well as the wealth of specific cross-modal correspondences and cognitive interactions between the senses attested in the psychological literature (e.g., Spence, 2011), the proposal of a hierarchy of the senses arguably has low a priori probability: it would be quite remarkable if the complex web of perceptual and linguistic connections between the senses would collapse into a simple divide between lower and higher senses, or a simple linear cline which indeed, our meta-analysis shows, is not the case. When seen from the perspective of this nonexhaustive list of differences between the senses, we should be skeptical about any claims that purport to have found *the* criterion that explains all observed asymmetries in linguistic synesthesia in one swoop, such as when Shen (1997) and Zhong et al. (2023) state that bodily contact is the key criterion. Moreover, we should also ask: How can we know that the right criterion has been picked; that is, what external evidence can be ascertained to put each criterion to a direct empirical test? For example, if touch, taste, and smell are supposed to be more "embodied" or "concrete" senses, how can we directly test this using empirical data without inviting circularity? And: Can we rule out that the other ways in which the senses differ in either perception or language do not also explain some of the patterns in linguistic synesthesia? That is, to the extent that "embodiment" is meant to be a defining feature that explains empirically observed asymmetries, this needs to be actively contrasted with other theoretical proposals. In fact, there already are empirical studies that show that dimensions other than "concreteness" or "embodiment" *do* help us explain generalizations about linguistic synesthesia, such as the composition of sensory vocabulary (Strik-Lievers, 2015; Winter, 2019a), or the affective loading (Winter, 2019a, Ch. 18), iconicity (Winter, 2019a, Ch. 18), or scalarity (Petersen et al., 2008) of sensory adjectives. This means that factors other than the hierarchy have already received direct empirical support. This is in stark contrast to any of the criteria used to motivate the hierarchy, which have to this date never been directly tested.

The passing mention of "among other interpretations" in the above quote also indexes another problem: theoretical malleability. The very same generalizations that Zhong et al. (2023) try to capture with their account has also been the explanatory target of the work by Shen and colleagues (Shen, 1997; Shen & Aisenman, 2008; Shen & Cohen, 1998; Shen & Gadir, 2009; Shen & Gil, 2008); yet, they propose slightly different criteria to motivate the hierarchy, such as "accessibility" or whether or not a sense is associated with a dedicated sensory organ. In fact, Winter (2019a) discusses how within the work of Shen and colleagues, the interpretation of the hierarchy has subtly shifted over successive publications (pp. 106–107). This is problematic because if anything external to language is supposed to help explain the generalizations about linguistic synesthesia observed in corpora or dictionaries, it cannot be the case that motivating factors can easily be swapped. Doing so perhaps exposes the fact that these proposals are largely post-hoc: criteria such as concreteness, accessibility, and embodiment are recruited to help make sense of the data, but they are not independently motivated, and hence do not have any predictive power.

Notice furthermore that the passage above offers only speculative interpretations of what "degrees of embodiment" may mean, such as distance to the body, or subjectivity, without spelling out why this would motivate the specific asymmetries observed in language: *what about distance or subjectivity* motivates source or target preference in linguistic synesthesia? If subjectivity is what explained asymmetries, we have to consider the fact that smell is a subjective sense par excellence, with little intersubjective agreement between people (see, e.g., Levinson & Majid, 2014; Majid & Burenhult, 2014). If we take subjectivity as motivating source preference, then smell would be expected to be a more likely source than even touch, which is not borne out by the data. If, on the other hand, bodily contact is such an important principle, why do Zhong et al. (2023) themselves classify smell as a "more embodied" sense (p. 2), given that smell, in contrast to both touch and taste, affords perception at a distance? All of this serves to show that proposals that characterize the senses in terms of broad notions such as "concreteness" or "embodiment" are often not spelled out in sufficient enough detail. To derive precise predictions from these accounts, proposals would have to explicitly position each of the five senses with respect to the proposed criteria; that is, how exactly do the different criteria add up to a divide between lower and higher senses, let alone a linear hierarchy?

Within cognitive linguistics, invoking "embodiment" loosely without spelling out the exact cognitive mechanisms has been problematized (Bergen, 2019), especially given the many different theoretical interpretations of "embodiment" (Wilson, 2002; Wilson & Golonka, 2013). Similarly, cognitive linguists have also problematized the fact that the notion of "concreteness" is often left undefined and assumed to be self-evident (Dunn, 2015), whereas in fact it is itself a notion that has received continuing debate in the literature on embodied cognition (Barsalou et al., 2018; Connell & Lynott, 2012; Dunn, 2015; Löhr, 2021; Lupyan & Winter, 2018; Winter, 2022). The standard definition of concreteness in cognitive science is that concreteness refers to "the degree to which the concept denoted by a word refers to a perceptible entity" (Brysbaert et al., 2014, p. 904), which is incongruent with the notion of concreteness referenced by proponents of the hierarchy of the senses, since all sensory properties are by definition concrete, in the standard sense of being accessible to the senses. Actually, if a distinction between the senses in terms of concreteness can be made at all, the widely used concreteness ratings by Brysbaert et al. (2014) do not conform to the description of the hierarchy above: Connell et al. (2018) show that words that are more visual are on average also rated to be more concrete ($r = 0.56$), more so than words that are more haptic ($r = 0.53$), olfactory ($r = 0.26$), and gustatory ($r = 0.16$). This data shows that native speaker intuitions do not coincide with the view that the senses differ in terms of concreteness in a way that is laid out by Zhong et al. (2023) or similar such accounts (e.g., Shen, 1997).

All of these known problems are ignored when a particular sensory modality is judged to be more or less "embodied," "accessible," or "concrete," whatever these terms may precisely mean when predicated on the five senses. It should also cause us worry that the notions linguists use to characterize linguistic synesthesia have no backing from those fields that most intimately study the senses, such as perceptual psychology and neuropsychology. For example, we would be hard-pressed to find any experiment in perceptual psychology that would allow lining up all of the five senses on a simple cline of "concreteness" or any similarly coarse criteria. In fact, the language-external motivations of the hierarchy proposed so far could be seen as being fundamentally at odds with the "cognitive commitment" of cognitive linguistics, which proposes that theories "must provide an account of mind that is cognitively and neurally realistic" (Lakoff & Johnson, 1999, pp. 79–80). Dąbrowska (2016) is concerned that researchers in cognitive linguistics often only "pay lip service" to the cognitive commitment, not always engaging with current studies in such fields as psychology, cognitive science, and neuroscience. This concern arguably directly applies to the literature on linguistic synesthesia, where, with few exceptions, we do not find detailed discussion of non-linguistic data (e.g., Ronga, 2016; Ronga et al., 2012). Without citing modern research in such fields as perceptual psychology or neuroscience, it is not clear how seriously we can take proposals that claim that touch, taste, and smell are somehow more "concrete" or "embodied" than sight and sound.

The above quote also tries to situate linguistic synesthesia within research on conceptual metaphor, which we deem to be a highly problematic theoretical move. Winter (2019a, pp. 85–86) discusses the fact that linguistic synesthesias look wholly unlike standard conceptual metaphors, such as THEORIES ARE BUILDINGS (Grady, 1997). As observed by Strik-Lievers (2017), linguistic synesthesia "may be distinguished from other metaphors because the conflicting concepts are both sensory, referring to two conceptually separate senses" (p. 97), whereas conceptual metaphor theory is largely concerned with mappings between domains or frames that are accessible to the senses to domains or frames that are inaccessible to the senses (Gibbs, 1994; Lakoff & Johnson, 1980, 1999). Distinguishing between different senses in terms of concreteness is neither part of standard definitions of concreteness in cognitive science nor part of how the concept is commonly characterized in conceptual metaphor theory. As it is not clear that differences between the senses can be adequately captured in terms of the coarse notion of "concreteness," it is not clear that the integration of linguistic synesthesia into conceptual metaphor theory is a fruitful theoretical endeavor. Moreover, we have to ask what the conceptual pay-off of such integration would be, given that asymmetries and patterns in linguistic synesthesia can already be described well without specifically invoking conceptual metaphor theory.

Finally, in stark contrast to conceptual metaphor theory, the notion of a hierarchy of the senses has not moved beyond basic circularity issues (for discussion, see Fishman, 2022; Winter, 2019a) known to frequently plague work in cognitive linguistics (Dąbrowska, 2016; Gibbs, 2007). Early debates in conceptual metaphor theory have been attacked on the grounds that conceptual mappings are inferred from patterns in linguistic data, which are then used to explain those very patterns (Murphy, 1996, 1997). To move conceptual metaphor theory out of this circularity trap, researchers have amassed empirical evidence showing that the same conceptual mappings evidenced in language also exist independently of language (e.g., Boroditsky, 2000; Casasanto & Boroditsky, 2008; Cienki & Müller, 2008; Gibbs, 1996, 2013; Winter & Matlock, 2013), and only thanks to such language-external data did the idea that conceptual metaphors underlie linguistic metaphors gain acceptance within the cognitive science community. When it comes to the principles that Shen (1997), Zhong et al. (2023), or others use to motivate the hierarchy, we have no such independent evidence. Instead, the hierarchy as a proposal appears to be derived from the data that it seeks to explain. Despite decades worth of empirical research, the hierarchy of the senses remains an elusive account, characterized by verbal statements that are open to different interpretations, that are insufficient in establishing linearity, and that use notions that are not grounded in external evidence backed up by studies from such fields as perceptual psychology or neuroscience. In fact, it is clear that what is supposed to motivate the hierarchy of the senses has never been genuinely tested, as it also is the case that studies are rarely set up to rule out alternative proposals (cf. Fishman, 2022).

Should we address these theoretical challenges, flesh out the proposals, and work on rescuing the hierarchy of the senses as a theoretical notion? Our meta-analysis here suggests that this may be a futile endeavor, simply because there is nothing in the data that genuinely lines up with existing proposals of the hierarchy of the senses in the first place. We should shift gears and consider that what is actually in need of an explanation are the generalizations (a–d) mentioned above.

9.4 Implications for Experimental Research

While our meta-analysis focuses on observational data, it also has direct implications for experimental research on linguistic synesthesia. First, as discussed in Section 2, the bulk of experimental research on linguistic synesthesia targets generalizations that stem from observational data: how linguistic synesthesia patterns in natural language. Several experiments in this space are designed to test the hierarchy of the senses using, for example, acceptability, comprehensibility, or naturalness judgments (Shen, 1997; Shen & Cohen, 1998; Shen & Gadir, 2009; Zhong et al., 2023). These experiments often follow the structure that participants' responses to stimuli with hierarchy-congruent mappings are compared to responses with hierarchy-incongruent mappings. Our meta-analysis directly speaks to these experiments in that it suggests that we should target a different set of generalizations about linguistic synesthesia, as outlined in (a–d) above.

On top of this, our results suggest that also in experimental research, we should pay more attention to individual mappings. Take, for example, Zhong et al.'s (2023) experiment, which found that novel metaphors congruent with the hierarchy, such as *silky sound* (touch→sound) and *shiny tune* (sight→sound), are more acceptable than those incongruent with the hierarchy, such as *rhythmic perfume* (sound→smell) or *hoarse taste* (sound→taste). Out of their 10 stimuli representing the hierarchy-congruent condition, they included 2 touch→sound, 3 sight→sound, 2 touch→sight, 2 taste→smell, and 1 touch→taste mappings. When juxtaposed with the results from our meta-analysis, we can see that 7 out of the 10 experimental stimuli are from precisely those mappings that we have also found to be particularly over-represented in the observational data (touch→sound, sight→sound, touch→sight). And just as was the case with our hierarchy congruency analysis, this means that the average condition difference found by Zhong et al. (2023) could be unduly affected by a small set of specific mappings. Moreover, we cannot take this experiment to confirm the hierarchy if important mappings are excluded, for example, taste→sound and taste→sight.

This concern applies not just to the composition of stimuli when setting up a study but also to how the experiment is analyzed after the data has been collected. In psycholinguistics, is has been standard for decades to model variation between items, for example, via random effects in mixed models (Baayen et al., 2008; Barr et al., 2013; Clark, 1973; Raaijmakers et al., 1999; Winter & Grice, 2021). Without including an item random effect, results do not formally generalize over items, and average results could easily stem from just one or two items driving the average. In stark contrast to standard practice in psycholinguistics, experimental research on linguistic synesthesia generally never considers items analyses (e.g., Fishman, 2022; Zhong et al., 2023), which means that these experiments do not allow drawing conclusions about linguistic synesthesia writ large and ultimately end up committing what is known as the "language-as-fixed-effect fallacy" (Clark, 1973). However, experimental research needs more than just random effects for specific items; it also needs to actively model variation between mappings. The way experiments are set up and analyzed now conceptually mirrors our analysis #1, the hierarchy congruency analysis. Because of this, we simply do not know whether results may hinge on a small subset of items, or particularly strong mappings. Without formally modeling item and mapping variation, strictly speaking, these experiments have failed to directly test the hierarchy. Our data suggests that future experiments on the hierarchy would have to include many more stimuli that include a more balanced set of those mappings supposed to be hierarchy-congruent, not just a small and potentially biased subset of mappings. And once data has been collected, variation between mappings and items needs to be explicitly incorporated into statistical models to allow generalization (cf. Winter & Grice, 2021).

10 Conclusion and Outlook for Future Research on Linguistic Synesthesia

We have found no support for the idea that there are preferences in linguistic synesthesia that can be interpreted as *forming* a linear directional hierarchy of the senses, nor as *reflecting* such a hierarchy. Our meta-analysis arrives at four specific generalizations, which in part echo Ullmann's original generalizations more so than modern-day reinterpretations of the hierarchy, which have become increasingly monolithic and linear over time. In line with our generalizations, we suggest that in both observational and experimental research, much more emphasis needs to be put on specific mappings. If our aim is to *explain* the patterns seen in the observational data, we may have been explaining the wrong tendencies, for example, thinking we need to "explain" a hierarchy when in fact the majority of cases attributed to this hierarchy come from a small set of mappings. To make progress in this field, we need to move beyond the cycle of confirming and reconfirming the hierarchy of the senses while ignoring or not accounting for the many exceptions and more nuanced patterns in the data. Theoretically, our results call for actively endorsing more network-based rather than hierarchical or linear representations of the connections between the senses, mirroring developments in the typological study of sensory language (Norcliffe & Majid, 2024), and other quantitative studies of sensory vocabulary (Hinojosa et al., 2020).

Researchers have begun to show how factors such as the composition of the sensory vocabulary (Strik-Lievers, 2015), or the emotional valence (Winter, 2019a, Ch. 17) and scalarity (Petersen et al., 2008) of sensory adjectives help explain some of the same asymmetries that the hierarchy is supposed to explain. This evidence, which already shows that more than the hierarchy is clearly at play, is often not discussed in studies focused on supporting the hierarchy. With this in mind, we worry that the hierarchy of the senses limits the scope of what researchers in this space can investigate. In purporting to have all the answers, the hierarchy kills further questioning. We hope to have shown that there is actually much more about linguistic synesthesia we do not know than discussions of the hierarchy make it out to be, which makes research on linguistic synesthesia an exciting field of inquiry, ripe with new discoveries. We also hope to have paved the way for future research on linguistic synesthesia by taking stock of the observational research conducted to this date, and by more clearly delineating the explanatory target.

References

Alvarado, J. A., Velasco, C., & Salgado, A. (2024). The organization of semantic associations between senses in language. *Language and Cognition*, *16*(4), 1588–1617. https://doi.org/10.1017/langcog.2024.19.

Auvray, M., & Spence, C. (2008). The multisensory perception of flavor. *Consciousness and Cognition*, *17*(3), 1016–1031. https://doi.org/10.1016/j.concog.2007.06.005.

Baayen, H., Davidson, D. J., & Bates, D. M. (2008). Mixed-effects modeling with crossed random effects for subjects and items. *Journal of Memory and Language*, *59*(4), 390–412.

Bagli, M. (2017). Tastes we've lived by: Taste metaphors in English. *Textus*, *30*(1), 33–48.

Barr, D. J., Levy, R., Scheepers, C., & Tily, H. J. (2013). Random effects structure for confirmatory hypothesis testing: Keep it maximal. *Journal of Memory and Language*, *68*(3), 255–278.

Barsalou, L. W., Dutriaux, L., & Scheepers, C. (2018). Moving beyond the distinction between concrete and abstract concepts. *Philosophical Transactions of the Royal Society B: Biological Sciences*, *373*(1752), 20170144. https://doi.org/10.1098/rstb.2017.0144.

Bentz, C., & Winter, B. (2014). Languages with more second language learners tend to lose nominal case. In S. Wichmann & J. Good (Eds.), *Quantifying Language Dynamics* (pp. 96–124). Brill.

Bergen, B. (2019). Embodiment. In E. Dąbrowska & D. Divjak (Eds.), *Cognitive linguistics: Foundations of language* (pp. 11–35). Mouton de Gruyter.

Bickel, B. (2011). Absolute and statistical universals. In P. C. Hogan (Ed.), *The Cambridge Encyclopedia of the Language Sciences* (pp. 77–79). Cambridge University Press.

Bickel, B. (2015). Distributional typology: Statistical inquiries into the dynamics of linguistic diversity. In B. Heine & H. Narrog (Eds.), *The Oxford Handbook of Linguistic Analysis* (2nd ed., pp. 901–924). Oxford University Press.

Boroditsky, L. (2000). Metaphoric structuring: Understanding time through spatial metaphors. *Cognition*, *75*(1), 1–28. https://doi.org/10.1016/S0010-0277(99)00073-6.

Bottini, R., & Casasanto, D. (2013). Space and time in the child's mind: Metaphoric or ATOMic? *Frontiers in Psychology*, *4*, 803.

Bretones-Callejas, C. B. (2001). Synaesthetic metaphors in English. *University of California at Berkeley & International Computer Science Institute Technical Report*. http://ftp.icsi.berkeley.edu/ftp/global/pub/techreports/2001/tr-01-008.pdf.

Brysbaert, M., Warriner, A. B., & Kuperman, V. (2014). Concreteness ratings for 40 thousand generally known English word lemmas. *Behavior Research Methods*, *46*(3), 904–911.

Bürkner, P.-C. (2017). brms: An R package for Bayesian multilevel models using Stan. *Journal of Statistical Software*, *80*(1), 1–28.

Carlson, N. R. (2010). *Physiology of Behavior* (10th ed.). Allyn & Bacon.

Casasanto, D., & Boroditsky, L. (2008). Time in the mind: Using space to think about time. *Cognition*, *106*(2), 579–593. https://doi.org/10.1016/j.cognition.2007.03.004.

Case, T. I., Repacholi, B. M., & Stevenson, R. J. (2006). My baby doesn't smell as bad as yours: The plasticity of disgust. *Evolution and Human Behavior*, *27*(5), 357–365. https://doi.org/10.1016/j.evolhumbehav.2006.03.003.

Catricalà, M. (2008). Fenomenologie sinestetiche tra retorica e pragmatica. *Studi e Saggi Linguistici*, *XLVI*, 7–62.

Cienki, A., & Müller, C. (Eds.). (2008). *Metaphor and Gesture* (Vol. 3). John Benjamins.

Clark, H. H. (1973). The language-as-fixed-effect fallacy: A critique of language statistics in psychological research. *Journal of Verbal Learning and Verbal Behavior*, *12*(4), 335–359.

Classen, C. (1993). *Worlds of Sense: Exploring the Senses in History and across Cultures*. Routledge.

Clayton, A. (2021). *Bernoulli's Fallacy: Statistical Illogic at the Crisis of Modern Science*. Columbia University Press. https://doi.org/10.7312/clay19994-008.

Cohen, J. (1994). The earth is round (p < .05). *American Psychologist*, *49*(12), 997. https://doi.org/10.1037/0003-066X.49.12.997.

Connell, L., & Lynott, D. (2012). Strength of perceptual experience predicts word processing performance better than concreteness or imageability. *Cognition*, *125*(3), 452–465.

Connell, L., Lynott, D., & Banks, B. (2018). Interoception: The forgotten modality in perceptual grounding of abstract and concrete concepts. *Philosophical Transactions of the Royal Society B: Biological Sciences*, *373*(1752), 20170143.

Cysouw, M. (2010). Dealing with diversity: Towards an explanation of NP-internal word order frequencies. *Linguistic Typology*, *14*(2–3), 253–286. https://doi.org/10.1515/lity.2010.010.

References

Dąbrowska, E. (2016). Cognitive Linguistics' seven deadly sins. *Cognitive Linguistics*, *27*(4), 479–491. https://doi.org/10.1515/cog-2016-0059.

Day, S. (1996). Synaesthesia and synaesthetic metaphors. *Psyche*, *2*(32), 1–16.

De Felice, I. (2014). La sinestesia nella poesia latina. *Studi e Saggi Linguistici*, *LII*(1), 61–107.

Deroy, O., & Spence, C. (2013). Why we are not all synesthetes (not even weakly so). *Psychonomic Bulletin & Review*, *20*(4), 643–664.

De Salazar, D. (2019). *La sinestesia. Configurazioni retoriche intersensoriali nella lingua letteraria romena*. Aracne.

Doetsch Kraus, U. (1992). *La sinestesia en la poesía española desde la Edad Media hasta mediados del siglo XIX. Un enfoque semántico*. Universidad de Navarra.

Dombi, E. (1974). Synaesthesia and poetry. *Poetics*, *3*(3), 23–44.

Dryer, M. S. (1992). The Greenbergian word order correlations. *Language*, *68*(1), 81–138. https://doi.org/10.1353/lan.1992.0028.

Dunn, J. (2015). Modeling abstractness and metaphoricity. *Metaphor and Symbol*, *30*(4), 259–289.

Dunn, M., Greenhill, S. J., Levinson, S. C., & Gray, R. D. (2011). Evolved structure of language shows lineage-specific trends in word-order universals. *Nature*, *473*(7345), 79–82. https://doi.org/10.1038/nature09923.

Evans, N., & Wilkins, D. (2000). In the mind's ear: The semantic extensions of perception verbs in Australian languages. *Language*, *76*(3), 546–592.

Fishman, A. (2022). The picture looks like my music sounds: Directional preferences in synesthetic metaphors in the absence of lexical factors. *Language and Cognition*, *14*(2), 208–227. https://doi.org/10.1017/langcog.2022.2.

Fónagy, I. (1963). *Die Metaphern in der Phonetik [Metaphors in Phonetics]*. Mouton de Gruyter.

Fujimoto, T. (2001). Nihongo-ni okeru gokan-o arawasu kyoukankaku keiyoushi-ni tsuite [On shynaesthetic adjectives representing five senses in Japanese]. *Nidaba*, *30*, 74–83.

Galac, Á., & Zayniev, D. (2023). Paths of linguistic synesthesia across cultures: A lexical analysis of conventionalized cross-sensory meaning extensions in Europe and Central Asia. *Cognitive Linguistic Studies*, *10*(2), 450–479. https://doi.org/10.1075/cogls.00108.gal.

Garg, A. X., Hackam, D., & Tonelli, M. (2008). Systematic review and meta-analysis: When one study is just not enough. *Clinical Journal of the American Society of Nephrology*, *3*(1), 253. https://doi.org/10.2215/CJN.01430307.

Gibbs, R. W. (1994). *The Poetics of Mind: Figurative Thought, Language, and Understanding*. Cambridge University Press.

Gibbs, R. W. (1996). Why many concepts are metaphorical. *Cognition*, *61*(3), 309–319. https://doi.org/10.1016/s0010-0277(96)00723-8.

Gibbs, R. W. (2007). Why cognitive linguists should care more about empirical methods. In M. Gonzalez-Marquez, I. Mittelberg, S. Coulson, & M. Spivey (Eds.), *Methods in Cognitive Linguistics* (pp. 2–18). John Benjamins.

Gibbs, R. W. (2013). Walking the walk while thinking about the talk: Embodied interpretation of metaphorical narratives. *Journal of Psycholinguistic Research*, *42*(4), 363–378. https://doi.org/10.1007/s10936-012-9222-6.

Gigerenzer, G. (2004). Mindless statistics. *The Journal of Socio-Economics*, *33*(5), 587–606. https://doi.org/10.1016/j.socec.2004.09.033.

Gigerenzer, G., Swijtink, Z., Porter, T., Daston, L., & Kruger, L. (1989). *The Empire of Chance: How Probability Changed Science and Everyday Life*. Cambridge University Press.

Goldinger, S. D., Papesh, M. H., Barnhart, A. S., Hansen, W. A., & Hout, M. C. (2016). The poverty of embodied cognition. *Psychonomic Bulletin & Review*, *23*(4), 959–978. https://doi.org/10.3758/s13423-015-0860-1.

Grady, J. (1997). Theories are buildings revisited. *Cognitive Linguistics*, *8*(4), 267–290.

Gurevitch, J., Koricheva, J., Nakagawa, S., & Stewart, G. (2018). Meta-analysis and the science of research synthesis. *Nature*, *555*(7695), Article 7695. https://doi.org/10.1038/nature25753.

Hehman, E., & Xie, S. Y. (2021). Doing better data visualization. *Advances in Methods and Practices in Psychological Science*, *4*(4), 25152459211045334. https://doi.org/10.1177/25152459211045334.

Hickok, G. (2014). *The Myth of Mirror Neurons: The Real Neuroscience of Communication and Cognition*. W.W. Norton.

Hinojosa, J. A., Haro, J., Magallares, S., Duñabeitia, J. A., & Ferré, P. (2020). Iconicity ratings for 10,995 Spanish words and their relationship with psycholinguistic variables. *Behavior Research Methods*, *53*(3), 1262–1275. https://doi.org/10.3758/s13428-020-01496-z.

Hoekstra, R., Morey, R. D., Rouder, J. N., & Wagenmakers, E.-J. (2014). Robust misinterpretation of confidence intervals. *Psychonomic Bulletin & Review*, *21*(5), 1157–1164. https://doi.org/10.3758/s13423-013-0572-3.

Huang, C.-R., & Xiong, J. (2019). Linguistic synaesthesia in Chinese. In C.-R. Huang, Z. Jing-Schmidt, & B. Meistererst (Eds.), *The Routledge Handbook of Chinese Applied Linguistics* (pp. 294–312). Routledge.

Jaeger, T. F., Graff, P., Croft, W., & Pontillo, D. (2011). Mixed effect models for genetic and areal dependencies in linguistic typology. *Linguistic Typology*, *15*(2), 281–319. https://doi.org/10.1515/lity.2011.021.

Jo, C. (2017). A corpus-based study on synesthesia in Korean ordinary language. In R. E. Roxas (Ed.), *Proceedings of the 31st Pacific Asia Conference on Language, Information and Computation* (pp. 249–254). University of the Philippines.

Jo, C. (2018). Synesthetic metaphors in Korean compound words. In B. Devereyx, E. Shutova, & C.-R. Huang (Eds.), *Proceedings of the Eleventh International Conference on Language Resources and Evaluation (LREC 2018)*. European Language Resources Association (ELRA).

Jo, C. (2019). A corpus-based analysis of synesthetic metaphors in Korean. *Linguistic Research*, *36*(3), 459–483. https://doi.org/10.17250/khisli.36.3.201912.005.

Jo, C. (2022). Linguistic synesthesia in Korean: Universality and variation. *SAGE Open*, *12*(3), 1–13. https://doi.org/10.1177/21582440221117804.

Johansson, N., Anikin, A., Carling, G., & Holmer, A. (2019). The typology of sound symbolism: Defining macro-concepts via their semantic and phonetic features. *Linguistic Typology*, *24*(2), 253–310.

Kay, M. (2021). tidybayes: Tidy data and geoms for Bayesian models. *R Package Version 3.0.1*. https://doi.org/10.5281/zenodo.1308151.

Koptjevskaja-Tamm, M., Miestamo, M., & Börstell, C. (2024). A cross-linguistic study of lexical and derived antonymy. *Linguistics*, *62*(6), 1417–1472. https://doi.org/10.1515/ling-2023-0140.

Kövecses, Z. (2002). *Metaphor: A Practical Introduction*. Oxford University Press.

Kumcu, A. (2021). Linguistic synesthesia in Turkish: A corpus-based study of crossmodal directionality. *Metaphor and Symbol*, *36*(4), 241–255. https://doi.org/10.1080/10926488.2021.1921557.

Lakoff, G., & Johnson, M. (1980). *Metaphors We Live By*. University of Chicago Press.

Lakoff, G., & Johnson, M. (1999). *Philosophy in the Flesh: The Embodied Mind and Its Challenge to Western Thought*. Basic Books.

Leshinskaya, A., & Caramazza, A. (2016). For a cognitive neuroscience of concepts: Moving beyond the grounding issue. *Psychonomic Bulletin & Review*, *23*(4), 991–1001. https://doi.org/10.3758/s13423-015-0870-z.

Levinson, S. C., & Majid, A. (2014). Differential ineffability and the senses. *Mind & Language*, *29*(4), 407–427. https://doi.org/10.1111/mila.12057.

Löhr, G. (2021). What are abstract concepts? On lexical ambiguity and concreteness ratings. *Review of Philosophy and Psychology*, *13*, 1–18. https://doi.org/10.1007/s13164-021-00542-9.

Lupyan, G., & Winter, B. (2018). Language is more abstract than you think, or, why aren't languages more iconic? *Philosophical Transactions of the Royal*

Society B: Biological Sciences, *373*(1752), 20170137. https://doi.org/10.1098/rstb.2017.0137.

Lynott, D., & Connell, L. (2009). Modality exclusivity norms for 423 object properties. *Behavior Research Methods*, *41*(2), 558–564.

Mahon, B. Z., & Caramazza, A. (2008). A critical look at the embodied cognition hypothesis and a new proposal for grounding conceptual content. *Journal of Physiology-Paris*, *102*(1), 59–70. https://doi.org/10.1016/j.jphysparis.2008.03.004.

Mahon, B. Z., & Hickok, G. (2016). Arguments about the nature of concepts: Symbols, embodiment, and beyond. *Psychonomic Bulletin & Review*, *23*(4), 941–958. https://doi.org/10.3758/s13423-016-1045-2.

Majid, A., & Burenhult, N. (2014). Odors are expressible in language, as long as you speak the right language. *Cognition*, *130*(2), 266–270. https://doi.org/10.1016/j.cognition.2013.11.004.

Majid, A., Roberts, S. G., Cilissen, L. et al. (2018). Differential coding of perception in the world's languages. *Proceedings of the National Academy of Sciences*, *115*(45), 11369–11376. https://doi.org/10.1073/pnas.1720419115.

Mancaș, M. (1962). La synesthésie dans la création artistique de M. Eminescu, T. Arghezi et M. Sadoveanu. *Cahiers de Linguistique Théorique et Appliquée*, *1*, 55–87.

Marks, L. E. (1974). On associations of light and sound: The mediation of brightness, pitch, and loudness. *The American Journal of Psychology*, *87*(1/2), 173–188. https://doi.org/10.2307/1422011.

Marks, L. E. (1978). *The Unity of the Senses: Interrelations among the Modalities*. Academic Press.

Marotta, G. (2011). Perché i colori chiassosi non fanno chiasso? Vincoli semantici e sintattici sulle associazioni sinestetiche. *Archivio Glottologico Italiano*, *XCVI*(2), 195–220. https://doi.org/10.1400/206836.

Marotta, G. (2012). Sinestesie tra vista, udito e dintorni: Un'analisi semantica distribuzionale. In M. Catricalà (Ed.), *Sinestesie e monoestesie: Prospettive a confronto* (pp. 19–51). Franco Angeli.

McElreath, R. (2020). *Statistical Rethinking: A Bayesian Course with Examples in R and Stan* (2nd ed.). CRC Press.

Morey, R. D., Hoekstra, R., Rouder, J. N., Lee, M. D., & Wagenmakers, E.-J. (2016). The fallacy of placing confidence in confidence intervals. *Psychonomic Bulletin & Review*, *23*(1), 103–123. https://doi.org/10.3758/s13423-015-0947-8.

Morey, R. D., Kaschak, M. P., Díez-Álamo, A. M. et al. (2021). A pre-registered, multi-lab non-replication of the action-sentence compatibility effect (ACE). *Psychonomic Bulletin & Review*, *29*, 613–626. https://doi.org/10.3758/s13423-021-01927-8.

Murphy, G. L. (1996). On metaphoric representation. *Cognition*, *60*(2), 173–204. https://doi.org/10.1016/0010-0277(96)00711-1.

Murphy, G. L. (1997). Reasons to doubt the present evidence for metaphoric representation. *Cognition*, *62*(1), 99–108. https://doi.org/10.1016/S0010-0277(96)00725-1.

Nakamura, T., Sakamoto, M., & Utsumi, A. (2010). The role of event knowledge in comprehending synesthetic metaphors. In S. Ohlsson & R. Catrambone (Eds.), *Proceedings of the Annual Meeting of the 32nd Annual Meeting of the Cognitive Science Society* (Vol. 32, pp. 1898–1903). Cognitive Science Society.

Norcliffe, E., & Majid, A. (2024). Verbs of perception: A quantitative typological study. *Language*, *100*(1), 81–123.

O'Boyle, M. W., & Tarte, R. D. (1980). Implications for phonetic symbolism: The relationship between pure tones and geometric figures. *Journal of Psycholinguistic Research*, *9*(6), 535–544. https://doi.org/10.1007/BF01068115.

Ortega, L., Guzman-Martinez, E., Grabowecky, M., & Suzuki, S. (2014). Audition dominates vision in duration perception irrespective of salience, attention, and temporal discriminability. *Attention, Perception, & Psychophysics*, *76*(5), 1485–1502. https://doi.org/10.3758/s13414-014-0663-x.

Paissa, P. (1995). *La sinestesia: Analisi contrastiva delle sinestesie lessicalizzate nel codice italiano e francese*. La Scuola.

Paradis, C., & Eeg-Olofsson, M. (2013). Describing sensory experience: The genre of wine reviews. *Metaphor and Symbol*, *28*(1), 22–40. https://doi.org/10.1080/10926488.2013.742838.

Pedersen, T. L. (2020). *Patchwork: The Composer of Plots*. https://CRAN.R-project.org/package=patchwork.

Perezgonzalez, J. D. (2015). Fisher, Neyman-Pearson or NHST? A tutorial for teaching data testing. *Frontiers in Psychology*, *6*, 223. https://doi.org/10.3389/fpsyg.2015.00223.

Petersen, W., Fleischhauer, J., Beseoglu, H., & Bücker, P. (2008). A frame-based analysis of synaesthetic metaphors. *The Baltic International Yearbook of Cognition, Logic and Communication*, *3*(1), 122.

Popova, Y. (2005). Image schemas and verbal synaesthesia. In B. Hampe (Ed.), *From Perception to Meaning: Image Schemas in Cognitive Linguistics* (Vol. 29, pp. 395–419). Mouton de Gruyter.

Prandi, M. (2023). Is figurative interpretation an outcome of ambiguity? *International Journal of Language Studies*, *17*(3), 21–36.

R Core Team. (2019). *R: A Language and Environment for Statistical Computing*. R Foundation for Statistical Computing.

Raaijmakers, J. G. W., Schrijnemakers, J. M. C., & Gremmen, F. (1999). How to deal with "The Language-as-Fixed-Effect Fallacy": Common misconceptions and alternative solutions. *Journal of Memory and Language*, *41*(3), 416–426. https://doi.org/10.1006/jmla.1999.2650.

Rakova, M. (2003). *The Extent of the Literal: Metaphor, Polysemy and Theories of Concepts*. Palgrave Macmillan.

Roberts, S., & Winters, J. (2013). Linguistic diversity and traffic accidents: Lessons from statistical studies of cultural traits. *PloS One*, *8*(8), e70902. https://doi.org/10.1371/journal.pone.0070902.

Roberts, S., Winters, J., & Chen, K. (2015). Future tense and economic decisions: Controlling for cultural evolution. *PloS One*, *10*(7), e0132145.

Ronga, I. (2016). Taste synaesthesias: Linguistic features and neurophysiological bases. In E. Gola & F. Ervas (Eds.), *Metaphor and Communication* (pp. 47–60). John Benjamins.

Ronga, I., Bazzanella, C., Rossi, F., & Iannetti, G. (2012). Linguistic synaesthesia, perceptual synaesthesia, and the interaction between multiple sensory modalities. *Pragmatics & Cognition*, *20*(1), 135–167.

Rosiello, L. (1963). Le sinestesie nell'opera poetica di Montale. *Rendiconti*, *7*, 1–19.

Rozeboom, W. W. (1960). The fallacy of the null-hypothesis significance test. *Psychological Bulletin*, *57*(5), 416. https://doi.org/10.1037/h0042040.

Saitis, C., & Weinzierl, S. (2019). The semantics of timbre. In K. Siedenburg, C. Saitis, S. McAdams, A. N. Popper, & R. R. Fay (Eds.), *Timbre: Acoustics, Perception, and Cognition* (pp. 119–149). Springer.

Sakamoto, M., & Utsumi, A. (2014). Adjective metaphors evoke negative meanings. *PloS One*, *9*(2), e89008. https://doi.org/10.1371/journal.pone.0089008.

Salzmann, K. (2014). Lexikalisierte Synästhesien im Sprachvergleich Italienisch-Deutsch. *Studi e Saggi Linguistici*, *LII*(1), 109–140.

Sandler, W., & Lillo-Martin, D. (2006). *Sign Language and Linguistic Universals*. Cambridge University Press.

Sanz-Valdivieso, L., & López-Arroyo, B. (2024). Figurative language and sensory perception: Corpus-based computer-assisted study of the nature and motivation of synesthetic metaphors in olive oil tasting notes. *Metaphor and Symbol*, *39*(4), 260–280. https://doi.org/10.1080/10926488.2024.2377535.

Schmidt, F. L. (1992). What do data really mean? Research findings, meta-analysis, and cumulative knowledge in psychology. *American*

Psychologist, *47*(10), 1173–1181. https://doi.org/10.1037/0003-066X.47.10.1173.

Shams, L., Kamitani, Y., & Shimojo, S. (2000). What you see is what you hear. *Nature*, *408*(6814), Article 6814. https://doi.org/10.1038/35048669.

Shen, Y. (1997). Cognitive constraints on poetic figures. *Cognitive Linguistics*, *8*(1), 33–72. https://doi.org/10.1515/cogl.1997.8.1.33.

Shen, Y., & Aisenman, R. (2008). Heard melodies are sweet, but those unheard are sweeter': Synaesthetic metaphors and cognition. *Language and Literature*, *17*(2), 107–121. https://doi.org/10.1177/0963947007088222.

Shen, Y., & Cohen, M. (1998). How come silence is sweet but sweetness is not silent: A cognitive account of directionality in poetic synaesthesia. *Language and Literature*, *7*(2), 123–140. https://doi.org/10.1177/096394709800700202.

Shen, Y., & Gadir, O. (2009). How to interpret the music of caressing: Target and source assignment in synaesthetic genitive constructions. *Journal of Pragmatics*, *41*(2), 357–371. https://doi.org/10.1016/j.pragma.2008.08.002.

Shen, Y., & Gil, D. (2008). Sweet fragrances from Indonesia: A universal principle governing directionality in synaesthetic metaphors. In J. Auracher, & W. van Peer (Eds.), *New Beginnings in Literary Studies* (pp. 49–71). Cambridge Scholars Publishing.

Shinohara, K., & Nakayama, A. (2011). Modalities and directions in synaesthetic metaphors in Japanese. *Cognitive Studies*, *18*(3), 491–507. https://doi.org/10.11225/jcss.18.491.

Simner, J., Harrold, J., Creed, H., Monro, L., & Foulkes, L. (2009). Early detection of markers for synaesthesia in childhood populations. *Brain*, *132*(1), 57–64. https://doi.org/10.1093/brain/awn292.

Simner, J., Mulvenna, C., Sagiv, N. et al. (2006). Synaesthesia: The prevalence of atypical cross-modal experiences. *Perception*, *35*(8), 1024–1033. https://doi.org/10.1068/p5469.

Sóskuthy, M., & Roettger, T. B. (2020). When the tune shapes morphology: The origins of vocatives. *Journal of Language Evolution*, *5*(2), 140–155. https://doi.org/10.1093/jole/lzaa007.

Speelman, C., & McGann, M. (2013). How mean is the mean? *Frontiers in Psychology*, *4*, 1–12. https://doi.org/10.3389/fpsyg.2013.00451.

Spence, C. (2011). Crossmodal correspondences: A tutorial review. *Attention, Perception, & Psychophysics*, *73*(4), 971–995. https://doi.org/10.3758/s13414-010-0073-7.

Strik-Lievers, F. (2015). Synaesthesia: A corpus-based study of cross-modal directionality. *Functions of Language*, *22*(1), 69–95.

Strik-Lievers, F. (2016). Synaesthetic metaphors in translation. *Studi e Saggi Linguistici*, *54*(1), 43–70.

Strik-Lievers, F. (2017). Figures and the senses. *Review of Cognitive Linguistics*, *15*(1), 83–101. https://doi.org/10.1075/rcl.15.1.04str.

Strik-Lievers, F. (2018). Synaesthesia and other figures: What the senses tell us about figurative language. In A. Baicchi, R. Digonnet, & J. L. Sandford (Eds.), *Sensory Perceptions in Language, Embodiment and Epistemology* (pp. 193–207). Springer.

Strik-Lievers, F. (2023). Synesthesia and language. In M. Aronoff (Ed.), *Oxford Bibliographies in Linguistics*. Oxford University Press. https://doi.org/10.1093/OBO/9780199772810-0307.

Strik-Lievers, F., & Huang, C.-R. (2016). A lexicon of perception for the identification of synaesthetic metaphors in corpora. In N. Calzolari, K. Choukri, T. Declerck, et al. (Eds.), *Proceedings of the Tenth International Conference on Language Resources and Evaluation (LREC'16)* (pp. 2270–2277). European Language Resources Association (ELRA). https://aclanthology.org/L16-1360.

Strik-Lievers, F., & Winter, B. (2018). Sensory language across lexical categories. *Lingua*, *204*, 45–61.

Torchiano, M. (2019). effsize: Efficient effect size computation. *R package Version 0.8.1*. https://doi.org/10.5281/zenodo.1480624.

Ullmann, S. (1937). Synaesthetic metaphors in William Morris. (An essay on the decorative art of the pre-Raphaelites). *Angol Filológiai Tanulmányok/Hungarian Studies in English*, *2*, 143–151.

Ullmann, S. (1945). Romanticism and synaesthesia: A comparative study of sense transfer in Byron and Keats. *Publications of the Modern Language Association of America*, *60*(3), 811–827. https://doi.org/10.2307/459180.

Ullmann, S. (1946). Les transpositions sensorielles chez Leconte de Lisle. *Le Français Moderne*, *14*, 23–40.

Ullmann, S. (1947). L'art de la transposition dans la poésie de Théophile Gautier. *Le Français Moderne*, *XV*, 265–286.

Ullmann, S. (1959). *The Principles of Semantics*. Jackson, Son.

Urban, M. (2011). Asymmetries in overt marking and directionality in semantic change. *Journal of Historical Linguistics*, *1*(1), 3–47.

Urbanek, S. (2022). *Png: Read and Write PNG Images*. https://CRAN.R-project.org/package=png.

Vasishth, S., & Nicenboim, B. (2016). Statistical methods for linguistic research: Foundational ideas – Part I. *Language and Linguistics Compass*, *10*(8), 349–369. https://doi.org/10.1111/lnc3.12201.

Vehtari, A., Gelman, A., & Gabry, J. (2017). Practical Bayesian model evaluation using leave-one-out cross-validation and WAIC. *Statistics and Computing, 27*(5), 1413–1432. https://doi.org/10.1007/s11222-016-9696-4.

Viberg, Å. (1983). The verbs of perception: A typological study. *Linguistics, 21*(1), 123–162.

Viberg, Å. (2001). The verbs of perception. In M. Haspelmath, E. König, W. Oesterreicher, & W. Raible (Eds.), *Language Universals* (pp. 1294–1309). Mouton de Gruyter.

Wallmark, Z. (2019). A corpus analysis of timbre semantics in orchestration treatises. *Psychology of Music, 47*(4), 585–605. https://doi.org/10.1177/0305735618768102.

Wallmark, Z., & Kendall, R. A. (2018). Describing sound: The cognitive linguistics of timbre. In E. I. Dolan & A. Rehding (Eds.), *The Oxford Handbook of Timbre*. Oxford University Press. https://doi.org/10.1093/oxfordhb/9780190637224.013.14.

Weissgerber, T. L., Milic, N. M., Winham, S. J., & Garovic, V. D. (2015). Beyond bar and line graphs: Time for a new data presentation paradigm. *PLoS Biology, 13*(4), e1002128. https://doi.org/10.1371/journal.pbio.1002128.

Werning, M., Fleischhauer, J., & Beseoglu, H. (2006). The cognitive accessibility of synaesthetic metaphors. In S. Ron & M. Naomi (Eds.), *Proceedings of the 28th Annual Conference of the Cognitive Science Society* (pp. 2365–2370). Lawrence Erlbaum Associates.

Whitney, A. H. (1952). Synaesthesia in twentieth-century Hungarian poetry. *The Slavonic and East European Review, 30*(75), 444–464.

Wickham, H., Averick, M., Bryan, J. et al. (2019). Welcome to the Tidyverse. *Journal of Open Source Software, 4*(43), 1686. https://doi.org/10.21105/joss.01686.

Williams, J. M. (1976). Synaesthetic adjectives: A possible law of semantic change. *Language, 52*(2), 461–478.

Wilson, A. D., & Golonka, S. (2013). Embodied cognition is not what you think it is. *Frontiers in Psychology, 4*, 58. https://doi.org/10.3389/fpsyg.2013.00058.

Wilson, M. (2002). Six views of embodied cognition. *Psychonomic Bulletin & Review, 9*(4), 625–636. https://doi.org/10.3758/BF03196322.

Winter, B. (2016). Taste and smell words form an affectively loaded and emotionally flexible part of the English lexicon. *Language, Cognition and Neuroscience, 31*(8), 975–988.

Winter, B. (2019a). *Sensory Linguistics: Language, Perception, and Metaphor*. John Benjamins.

Winter, B. (2019b). Synaesthetic metaphors are neither synaesthetic nor metaphorical. In L. J. Speed, C. O'Meara, L. San Roque, & A. Majid (Eds.), *Perception Metaphor* (pp. 105–126). John Benjamins.

Winter, B. (2022). Abstract concepts and emotion: Cross-linguistic evidence and arguments against affective embodiment. *Philosophical Transactions of the Royal Society B: Biological Sciences*, *378*(1870), 20210368. https://doi.org/10.1098/rstb.2021.0368.

Winter, B., & Grice, M. (2021). Independence and generalizability in linguistics. *Linguistics*, *59*(5), 1251–1277. https://doi.org/10.1515/ling-2019-0049.

Winter, B., Marghetis, T., & Matlock, T. (2015). Of magnitudes and metaphors: Explaining cognitive interactions between space, time, and number. *Cortex*, *64*, 209–224.

Winter, B., & Matlock, T. (2013). More is up . . . and right: Random number generation along two axes. *Proceedings of the Annual Meeting of the Cognitive Science Society*, *35*, 3789–3794.

Winter, B., Perlman, M., & Majid, A. (2018). Vision dominates in perceptual language: English sensory vocabulary is optimized for usage. *Cognition*, *179*, 213–220.

Winter, B., Sóskuthy, M., Perlman, M., & Dingemanse, M. (2022). Trilled /r/ is associated with roughness, linking sound and touch across spoken languages. *Scientific Reports*, *12*, 1035. https://doi.org/10.1038/s41598-021-04311-7.

Winter, B., & Srinivasan, M. (2021). Why is semantic change asymmetric? The role of concreteness and word frequency in metaphor and metonymy. *Metaphor and Symbol*, *37*(1), 39–54. https://doi.org/10.1080/10926488.2021.1945419.

Winter, B., & Strik-Lievers, F. (2023). Semantic distance predicts metaphoricity and creativity judgments in synesthetic metaphors. *Metaphor and the Social World*, *13*(1), 59–80. https://doi.org/10.1075/msw.00029.win.

Wnuk, E., & Majid, A. (2014). Revisiting the limits of language: The odor lexicon of Maniq. *Cognition*, *131*(1), 125–138. https://doi.org/10.1016/j.cognition.2013.12.008.

Youn, H., Sutton, L., Smith, E. et al. (2016). On the universal structure of human lexical semantics. *Proceedings of the National Academy of Sciences*, *113*(7), 1766–1771. https://doi.org/10.1073/pnas.1520752113.

Yu, N. (2003). Synesthetic metaphor: A cognitive perspective. *Journal of Literary Semantics*, *32*(1), 19–34. https://doi.org/10.1515/jlse.2003.001.

Zawisławska, M. (2019). *Metaphor and Senses. The Synamet Corpus: A Polish Resource for Synesthetic Metaphors*. Peter Lang.

Zhao, Q., Ahrens, K., & Huang, C.-R. (2022). Linguistic synesthesia is metaphorical: A lexical-conceptual account. *Cognitive Linguistics*, *33*(3), 553–583. https://doi.org/10.1515/cog-2021-0098.

Zhao, Q., Huang, C.-R., & Ahrens, K. (2019). Directionality of linguistic synesthesia in Mandarin: A corpus-based study. *Lingua*, *232*, 102744. https://doi.org/10.1016/j.lingua.2019.102744.

Zhao, Q., Long, Y., Jiang, X. et al. (2024). Linguistic synesthesia detection: Leveraging culturally enriched linguistic features. *Natural Language Processing*, 1–23. https://doi.org/10.1017/nlp.2024.9.

Zhong, Y., Ahrens, K., & Huang, C.-R. (2023). Novel metaphor and embodiment: Comprehending novel synesthetic metaphors. *Linguistics Vanguard*, *9*(1), 245–255. https://doi.org/10.1515/lingvan-2022-0020.

Acknowledgments

We thank Kazuko Shinohara for helping us with Japanese articles on linguistic synesthesia. We thank the three reviewers for their exceptionally constructive feedback on our original submission. Bodo Winter has been supported by the UKRI Future Leaders Fellowship (MR/T040505/1). We thank the audience of Figurative Thought and Language 2024 in Genoa for helpful comments and suggestions. All errors remain our own.

Cambridge Elements

Cognitive Linguistics

Sarah Duffy
Northumbria University

Sarah Duffy is Senior Lecturer in English Language and Linguistics at Northumbria University. She has published primarily on metaphor interpretation and understanding, and her forthcoming monograph for Cambridge University Press (co-authored with Michele Feist) explores *Time, Metaphor, and Language* from a cognitive science perspective. Sarah is Review Editor of the journal, *Language and Cognition*, and Vice President of the UK Cognitive Linguistics Association.

Nick Riches
Newcastle University

Nick Riches is a Senior Lecturer in Speech and Language Pathology at Newcastle University. His work has investigated language and cognitive processes in children and adolescents with autism and developmental language disorders, and he is particularly interested in usage-based accounts of these populations.

Editorial Board
Heng Li, *Southwest University*
John Newman, *University of Alberta (Edmonton)*
Kimberley Pager-McClymont, *University of Huddersfield*
Katie J. Patterson, *Universidad de Granada*
Maria Angeles Ruiz-Moneva, *University of Zaragoza*
Lexi Webster, *Manchester Metropolitan University*
Xu Wen, *Southwest University*

About the Series

Cambridge Elements in Cognitive Linguistics aims to extend the theoretical and methodological boundaries of cognitive linguistics. It will advance and develop established areas of research in the discipline, as well as address areas where it has not traditionally been explored and areas where it has yet to become well-established.

Cambridge Elements

Cognitive Linguistics

Elements in the Series

Language Change and Cognitive Linguistics: Case Studies from the History of Russian
Tore Nesset

Navigating the Realities of Metaphor and Psychotherapy Research
Dennis Tay

The Many Faces of Creativity: Exploring Synaesthesia through a Metaphorical Lens
Sarah Turner and Jeannette Littlemore

Metaphor, Metonymy, the Body and the Environment: An Exploration of the Factors That Shape Emotion-Colour Associations and Their Variation across Cultures
Jeannette Littlemore, Marianna Bolognesi, Nina Julich-Warpakowski, Chung-hong Danny Leung and Paula Pérez Sobrino

Applied Cognitive Linguistics and L2 Instruction
Reyes Llopis-García

Cognitive Linguistics and Language Evolution
Michael Pleyer and Stefan Hartmann

Computational Construction Grammar: A Usage-Based Approach
Jonathan Dunn

Signed Language and Cognitive Grammar
Sherman Wilcox, Rocío Martínez and Sara Siyavoshi

Linguistic Synesthesia: A Meta-analysis
Bodo Winter and Francesca Strik-Lievers

A full series listing is available at: www.cambridge.org/ECOG

For EU product safety concerns, contact us at Calle de José Abascal, 56–1°, 28003 Madrid, Spain or eugpsr@cambridge.org.

www.ingramcontent.com/pod-product-compliance
Ingram Content Group UK Ltd.
Pitfield, Milton Keynes, MK11 3LW, UK
UKHW021125180725
460934UK00013B/144